PSALMS

PSALMS

Reading and Studying the Book of Praises

W. H. BELLINGER, JR.

HENDRICKSON
PUBLISHERS
PEABODY, MASSACHUSETTS 01961-3473

For Libby

ISBN 0-943575-35-4

Second printing, November 1992

Library of Congress Cataloging-in-Publication Data

Bellinger, W. H.
    Psalms: reading and studying the book of praises / W.H.
Bellinger, Jr.
        p.   cm.
    Includes bibliographical references and indexes.
    ISBN 0-943575-35-4
    1. Bible. O.T. Psalms—Criticism, interpretation, etc.
I. Title
BS1430.2.B436   1990
223'.206—dc20   90-40913
                                                                  CIP

Table of Contents

Abbreviations

ANET	*Ancient Near Eastern Texts Relating to the Old Testament*
BJRL	*Bulletin of the John Rylands Library*
CBQ	*Catholic Biblical Quarterly*
JBL	*Journal of Biblical Literature*
JSOT	*Journal for the Study of the Old Testament*
JSOTS	*Journal for the Study of the Old Testament Supplement Series*
JSS	*Journal of Semitic Studies*
NCB	New Century Bible Commentary
OTL	Old Testament Library
SBLDS	Society of Biblical Literature Dissertation Series
SJT	*Scottish Journal of Theology*

Preface

Most of my professional life has focused on the book of Psalms. These poems center on worship and provide an especially fruitful source of insight concerning the relationship of theology and worship. My own pilgrimage keeps returning to just these concerns; many other readers of the Bible give testimony to similar experiences. Out of that background, I have written this book.

While ministers and other members of the worshiping community may find the volume useful, its primary intended audience is students. The aids at the end of the book should help that audience. I hope the work will be not a book about the Psalms, but a guide to reading and hearing the Psalms. The volume is well suited for reading in conjunction with the Psalms.

Producing a book leaves one indebted to many people. I wish to thank Baylor University, its President, the Dean of the College of Arts and Sciences, and my colleagues in the Department of Religion for providing a setting in which to study and write. The work for this volume has been supported significantly by the Baylor University Research Committee and by the Southwest Commission on Religious Studies. Many individuals have helped: Mikeal Parsons, Tony Moyers, Jan Granowski, Jann Clanton, Ronald Clements, and Sandra Ratley. I am also grateful to Patrick Alexander and Hendrickson Publishers. My wife, Libby, and children, Jill and Chip, have given me support.

I dedicate the volume to my wife, Elizabeth Smith Bellinger, faithful lover, companion, and friend. She makes possible every aspect of my life, and she has, no doubt, lived with the Psalms longer than she ever thought possible. I am grateful.

Getting Started

1

The book of Psalms is the most read, the most used, of all the Old Testament books. In the Psalms, ancient worshipers address God; for centuries people of faith have learned from these texts how to pray. The Psalms express every emotion—from joy to despair, from hate to love. Thus pilgrims of faith find themselves in the Psalms, and they find themselves praying. "Prayer Book of the Bible" is a fitting title for the book. Martin Luther wrote,

> This explains, moreover, why the Psalter is the favourite book of all the saints, and why each one of them, whatever his [sic] circumstances may be, finds in it psalms and words which are appropriate to the circumstances in which he finds himself and meet his needs as adequately as if they were composed exclusively for his sake.[1]

Many readers will fondly remember the Twenty-third Psalm: "The LORD is my shepherd; I shall not want. . . ." Or Psalm 100:

> Make a joyful noise to the LORD, all the lands!
> Serve the LORD with gladness!
> Come into his presence with singing! (vv. 1, 2)

Or Psalm 119:105: "Thy word is a lamp to my feet and a light

---

[1]See A. Weiser, *The Psalms* (OTL; Philadelphia: Westminster, 1962), 20.

to my path." People of faith throughout the generations, then, identify with the book of Psalms.

The Psalms have also significantly influenced history and theology. These texts relate to vital parts of the history of ancient Israel, and thus found a place in the life of the early church (Col 3:16; Eph 5:19; Mark 14:26). The book also forms a kind of summary of Old Testament theology, reflecting representative themes in the story of God and ancient Israel.[2] In addition the Psalms have influenced the worship of the church; they address the encounter between God and congregation as well as the significance of the worship event for the life of faith.

The Psalms have greatly affected the community of faith.[3] That reality alone moves us to study these texts to discover their historical impact and their relevance for contemporary life. We will begin with three introductory matters—setting, shape, poetry—that will prepare us to develop and apply a method of psalm study.

The Setting of the Psalter

Crucial to our study of the Psalms is a framework, and the setting in which Old Testament psalms occur can supply it. The narrative portions of the Old Testament contain psalms; such songs relate to specific experiences in the life of ancient Israel. Exodus 15:1–18 illustrates this. God has just delivered the people from oppression in Egypt, specifically from the armed forces of the Pharaoh at the sea. The people celebrate this deliverance with a hymn of praise:

> I will sing to the LORD, for he has triumphed
> gloriously;
> the horse and his rider he has thrown into the sea.

---

[2]See G. W. Anderson, "Israel's Creed: Sung not Signed," *SJT* 16 (1963): 277–85.

[3]Nazi concentration camp victims who found hope and strength in the Psalms provide recent history's best known illustration. See, for example, B. W. Anderson, *Out of the Depths* (Revised and expanded ed.; Philadelphia: Westminster, 1983), 14–15.

The LORD is my strength and my song,
    and he has become my salvation;
this is my God, and I will praise him,
    my father's God, and I will exalt him.
The LORD is a man of war;
    the LORD is his name. (vv. 1–3)

The psalm conveys the people's faith and helps them define and understand their encounter with God at this high point in their history. Other psalms embedded in the narrative parts of the Old Testament can also function as songs of faith:

1. Judges 5:1–31 celebrates God's victory for ancient Israel over the Canaanites. The song serves as a reminder of the God who delivers.
2. First Samuel 2:1–10 offers thanksgiving on the part of Hannah, who has just received the gift of a son. The song encourages future Israelite generations to have faith in the God who "raises up the poor from the dust" (v. 8).
3. Jonah 2:2–9 expresses thanksgiving for Jonah's deliverance from drowning, a deliverance wrought by way of the great fish. The psalm teaches that "Deliverance belongs to the LORD!" (v. 9) and that God is attentive to the cries of those in need.
4. Jeremiah 20:7–18 contains two of the prophet's prayers of lament. Jeremiah cried out in the midst of difficulty in his prophetic task. These prayers portray the painful side of the honest dialogue of faith and provide justification for the community's inclusion of the difficulties of life in its relationship with God. Jeremiah's laments also confronted ancient Israel with its refusal to repent in the face of God's word.

The Old Testament includes additional psalms, but these examples show that psalms function as pilgrimage songs, expressing and defining faith for the people of God.

The book of Psalms reflects the practice of the people journeying, going on a pilgrimage to worship in Jerusalem. We will see that there is a collection of psalms for the ascent to the temple. Note Psalm 122:1:

I was glad when they said to me,
"Let us go to the house of the LORD!"

People journeyed to Jerusalem for major festivals and sang psalms on the way.

We might also think of pilgrimage in a broader sense, as a metaphor for the life of faith. Believers, ancient and modern, journey through life. Psalms provided ancient Israel with expressions of faith to sing on the journey of life. Psalms kept the people going and expressed and defined their faith; such songs helped the people understand and enact their belief.

The Old Testament contributes this basic framework for reading psalms as songs of faith, but we also need to remember that the Old Testament has a broader setting—the ancient Near Eastern world. Writing psalms was an ancient practice. Archaeologists have discovered Mesopotamian, Canaanite, and Egyptian texts similar in language, poetic form, vocabulary, and thought to the psalms of the Old Testament. Hear a section from a hymn to the Assyrian Moon-God:

> O Lord, decider of the destinies of heaven and earth,
>   whose word no one alters,
> Who controls water and fire, leader of living creatures,
>   what god is like thee?
> In heaven who is exalted? Thou! Thou alone art exalted.
> On earth who is exalted? Thou! Thou alone art
>   exalted.[4]

Compare Ps 89:5–14:

> Let the heavens praise thy wonders, O LORD,
>   thy faithfulness in the assembly of the holy ones!
> For who in the skies can be compared to the LORD?
>   Who among the heavenly beings is like the LORD,
> a God feared in the council of the holy ones,
>   great and terrible above all that are round about him?
> O LORD God of hosts,
>   who is mighty as thou art, O LORD,
>   with thy faithfulness round about thee?
> Thou dost rule the raging of the sea;
>   when its waves rise, thou stillest them.

---

[4]"Hymn to the Moon-God," trans. F. J. Stephens, *ANET* (2d ed.; Princeton: Princeton University, 1955), 386.

Thou didst crush Rahab like a carcass,
  thou didst scatter thy enemies with thy mighty arm.
The heavens are thine, the earth also is thine;
  the world and all that is in it, thou hast founded
    them.
The north and south, thou hast created them;
  Tabor and Hermon joyously praise thy name.
Thou hast a mighty arm;
  strong is thy hand, high thy right hand.
Righteousness and justice are the foundation of thy
    throne;
  steadfast love and faithfulness go before thee.

Listen to part of a prayer of lamentation to Ishtar, the Queen of
Heaven:

How long, O my Lady, shall my adversaries be looking
    upon me,
In lying and untruth shall they plan evil against me,
Shall my pursuers and those who exult over me rage
    against me?
How long, O my Lady, shall the crippled and weak
    seek me out?
One has made for me long sackcloth; thus I have
    appeared before thee. . . .
Let my prayers and my supplications come to thee.
Let thy great mercy be upon me.
Let those who see me in the street magnify thy
    name.[5]

Compare Psalm 13:

How long, O LORD? Wilt thou forget me for ever?
  How long wilt thou hide thy face from me?
How long must I bear pain in my soul,
  and have sorrow in my heart all the day?
How long shall my enemy be exalted over me?
Consider and answer me, O LORD my God;
  lighten my eyes, lest I sleep the sleep of death;
lest my enemy say, "I have prevailed over him";
  lest my foes rejoice because I am shaken.

---

[5]"Prayer of Lamentation to Ishtar," trans. F. J. Stephens, *ANET*,
384–85.

> But I have trusted in thy steadfast love;
>   my heart shall rejoice in thy salvation.
> I will sing to the LORD,
>   because he has dealt bountifully with me.

Old Testament psalms also differ from other psalms in the ancient Near East. The immediate distinctiveness of Hebrew psalms is their vision of faith in the one God, Yahweh (the Lord). The book of Psalms is a central expression of ancient Israel's distinctive faith and as such encourages the community of faith to remain loyal to the one God, Yahweh. Psalm 29 demonstrates this. A number of scholars have argued that Psalm 29 betrays Canaanite influence. Some have suggested that this psalm is actually a Canaanite hymn that ancient Israel adapted to its faith; if this is true the psalm may even polemicize against the idols by saying that *Yahweh*, not the Canaanite nature deities, is to be praised as the Lord of nature.[6] To be sure, Psalm 29 *is* similar to other ancient Near Eastern texts, but it uniquely affirms ancient Israel's faith in the one God, Yahweh:

> The LORD sits enthroned over the flood;
>   the LORD sits enthroned as king for ever (v. 10).

Psalms, in short, come from a socio-historical setting in the ancient Near East and reflect Israel's encounter with God in that setting. Theology and culture interact in the Psalms as God uses the ancient Near Eastern setting as the medium and place of revelation. This reality implies that in ancient Israel the Psalms articulated faith and encouraged the people to hold fast during their pilgrimage of faith. The Psalms call for belief in Yahweh rather than in the Canaanite deities. Caution is essential for studying the ancient Near Eastern setting of the Old Testament and the Psalms, because we often are forced to depend on hypotheses. Nonetheless, an awareness of this background can help in reading the Psalter.

---

[6]For bibliography on the Canaanite background of Psalm 29, see P. C. Craigie, *Ugarit and the Old Testament* (Grand Rapids: Eerdmans, 1983), 68–71, 107–8.

Up to this point, the Old Testament setting of psalms and the ancient Near Eastern setting of the Old Testament have suggested a starting point for reading psalms—understanding them as pilgrimage songs of faith. The songs help articulate, encourage, and define belief in Yahweh; they help ancient Israel comprehend its distinctive faith. In the Hebrew Bible, the book of Psalms forms the standard collection of these texts. Therefore, we next need to inquire about the particular shape of that book.

The Shape of the Psalter

The organization of the book of Psalms is our next matter for consideration. We will look at the title, structure, superscriptions, and collections of the book of Psalms.

Title

The word "psalm" is a transliteration of the Greek word referring to a song performed to the accompaniment of stringed instruments. "Psalter" is another title for the book; this title comes from the Latin word indicating the stringed instrument used to accompany the songs. However, the original title of the book is the Hebrew סֵפֶר תְּהִלִּים (*sēper tĕhillîm*), "Book of Praises," a singularly appropriate title.

Structure

The Psalter consists of five divisions, or "books," analogous to the first five books of the Old Testament, the books of Moses. As there are five books of Moses, the Torah or Law, so there are five "books" of Psalms, perhaps in poetic response to the Torah:

FIVE BOOKS OF PSALMS	
Book I	Pss 1–41
Book II	Pss 42–72
Book III	Pss 73–89
Book IV	Pss 90–106
Book V	Pss 107–150

Each book ends with a benediction giving praise and thanksgiving to God, especially for the psalms just completed.

> Blessed be the LORD, the God of Israel,
>   from everlasting to everlasting!
>   Amen and Amen. (Ps 41:13)

See also Psalms 72:18–20; 89:52; 106:48; 150. Psalm 150 functions as a brief, powerful benediction for the fifth book of psalms and for the entire Psalter. The First Psalm forms the introduction to the Psalter, calling upon individuals to choose between two lifestyles—the way of the righteous or the way of the wicked. Psalm 2 is probably a second part of the introduction, because it concerns the same decision for nations. Psalm 149 speaks of the relation between Yahweh and the nations, as does Psalm 2; perhaps it is also part of the book's conclusion. The Psalter, then, traverses the path from obedience in righteous living to the uninhibited praise of Yahweh (Pss 149; 150), the response to the joy found in the lifestyle of righteousness.

Superscriptions

Of the 150 psalms, 116 have superscriptions, brief titles written just above the text. Most scholars agree that superscriptions are not original to the text but were added in the process of compiling the Psalter. Reasons for this judgment include: (1) the lack of agreement between the superscriptions in the Hebrew, Greek, and Syriac versions of the Old Testament; (2) analogy to other biblical texts, especially in Chronicles;[7] and (3) difficulties in correlating content in a given superscription[8] with that in the

---

[7]Chronicles, from the post-exilic era, does not fully reflect the practice of attaching superscriptions to psalms; the later Dead Sea Scrolls do, however. The practice thus probably derives from a time after the writing of Chronicles and before the production of the Dead Sea Scrolls.

[8]See, for example, B. S. Childs, "Psalm Titles and Midrashic Exegesis," *JSS* 16 (1971): 137–50; idem, *Introduction to the Old Testament as Scripture* (Philadelphia: Fortress, 1979), 520–22; O. Kaiser, *Introduction to the Old Testament* (Oxford: Basil Blackwell, 1975), 350–53; W. S. LaSor, D. A. Hubbard, and F. W. Bush, *Old Testament Survey* (Grand Rapids: Eerdmans, 1982), 528–30.

body of the corresponding psalm. Nonetheless, the superscriptions are a part of the book of Psalms and may hint about how ancient Israel interpreted these texts. The superscriptions vary but often contain three elements:

1. *Liturgical collections.* Many of the superscriptions contain a phrase such as "Psalm of David," "Psalm of Asaph," or "Psalm of the Sons of Korah," indicating the liturgical collection from which the psalm came. The compilers of the Psalter have used several collections. The next section discusses these.
2. *Technical terms related to use in worship.* Psalm 59 is a Miktam (golden poem) of David, and its superscription includes instructions to the choirmaster. The phrase "according to Do Not Destroy" apparently refers to the tune used to accompany the psalm. The meaning of some of these Hebrew terms is obscure, but they do appear to relate to the use of the psalm in worship.
3. *Historical notes.* Several psalm superscriptions include a setting for the psalm. The superscription of Psalm 59 says, "A Miktam of David, when Saul sent men to watch his house in order to kill him." These historical notes help the reader envision the psalm's impact in a particular setting in a representative person's life. These historical notes provide clues to the way the compilers of the Psalter understood certain psalms to function in life.

Psalm 57's superscription has all three elements: "To the choirmaster: according to Do Not Destroy [technical terms for use in worship]. A Miktam of David [liturgical collection], when he fled from Saul, in the cave [historical note]."

Collections

The Psalter contains several collections of psalms. Much interest has centered on the Psalms of David. Some suggest that the occurrence of the phrase, a psalm of David, in the superscription indicates Davidic authorship,[9] but the reference of the

---

[9]See, for example, E. W. Hengstenberg, *Commentary on the Psalms* (4th ed.; Edinburgh: T. & T. Clark, 1867); F. Delitzsch, *Biblical Commentary on the Psalms* (London: Hodder and Stoughton, 1902); A. F. Kirkpatrick, ed., *The Book of Psalms* (Cambridge Bible for Schools and Colleges; Cambridge: University Press; 1902).

Hebrew is less than clear. The Hebrew word contains the name "David," דָּוִד (*dāwid*) plus the preposition לְ (*lĕ*), which has a broad range of meanings: to, for, in relation to, in behalf of, belonging to. The superscriptions thus offer little basis for a decision about authorship. Other evidence suggests that the phrase indicates the liturgical collection or hymnbook from which the psalm came.

COLLECTIONS IN THE PSALTER	
Davidic Collections	Pss 3–41; 51–72; 138–145
Korahite Collections	Pss 42–49; 84–85; 87–88
Elohistic Collection	Pss 42–83
Asaphite Collection	Pss 73–83
Psalms on the Kingship of God	Pss 93–100
A Collection of Psalms of Praise	Pss 103–107
Songs of Ascents (Perhaps on ascent, pilgrimage, to the temple for worship)	Pss 120–134
Hallelujah Psalms (Beginning/ending with "hallelujah" [Praise the LORD])	Pss 111–118; 146–150

Other superscriptions refer to collections; this view accords well with the description of Asaph and the Sons of Korah in 1 and 2 Chronicles. "Of (belonging to) David" most likely refers to the psalm's original collection. The general nature of psalm language supports this view; the Psalms reflect representative life experiences rather than specific events in the life of one person. At the same time, the tradition relating David to the Psalms is strong and unmistakable in the Old Testament (1 Sam 16; 2 Sam 1; 22; 23; 1 Chr 16; 25; Amos 6). Perhaps we should say that David was the patron or the primary sponsor of psalmody in ancient

Israel. David gave important initial impetus to the writing of psalms and to their use in worship in Jerusalem. He may well have written psalms, but the Psalter provides little evidence on the question of authorship. It is clear, however, that David was the primary patron for psalm writing in ancient Israel, as was King James I for the King James Version of the Bible. A number of psalms come from the Davidic, royal collections, those collections given the royal stamp of approval for use in worship in Jerusalem.

Some Davidic psalms have become part of another collection, the Elohistic Psalter (Pss 42–83). This grouping of psalms gets its name from the dominant use of the name "Elohim," God, as opposed to the special Hebrew name "Yahweh," Lord, when referring to God. Additional evidence for the view that Psalms 42–83 formed an established collection comes to the fore when we realize that some psalms occur twice—once as a part of the Elohistic Psalter and elsewhere in the book of Psalms. For example, compare Psalm 14:2, 4 with Psalm 53:2, 4:

> The LORD looks down from heaven upon the children
> of men . . .
> Have they no knowledge, all the evildoers
> who eat up my people as they eat bread,
> and do not call upon the LORD? (Ps 14:2, 4,
> emphasis mine)

> God looks down from heaven upon the sons of
> men . . .
> Have those who work evil no understanding,
> who eat up my people as they eat bread,
> and do not call upon God? (Ps 53:2, 4, emphasis
> mine)

Psalm 40:13–17, when compared with Psalm 70, exhibits the same convention. In addition, the psalms of the Elohistic Psalter contain the phrase, "God your God," which is usually "Lord your God" (Pss 43:4; 45:7; 50:7; 68:8). For some reason, the compilers of this collection preferred the term "Elohim" for God. No one is sure why they preferred this title, but their work does show that Psalms 42–83 comprised an identifiable collection of psalms at some time.

We do not have a complete picture of the way these collections came together, but that they overlap shows the process involved in the final compilation of the Psalter. We will return to this issue in the next chapter, but some preliminary comments may help. The core of the Psalter is the Davidic collections (Pss 3–41; 51–72; 138–145), texts which are most often cries for help in the midst of crisis and which come from an individual rather than from the whole community. The psalms of the Sons of Korah (Pss 42–49; 84–85; 87–88) and the psalms of Asaph (Pss 73–83) include more community psalms. With the psalms on the kingship of God (Pss 93–100), the book begins to move toward the praise of God, a movement which continues in Books IV and V (see chart on p. 7). In sum, the Psalter is shaped in a purposeful way; that shape has come to us by way of a lengthy process.

This section has provided some basic information on the shape of the Psalter—its title, structure, superscriptions, and collections. Awareness of these matters can help us understand the Psalms.

The Poetry of the Psalter

Another significant matter to consider in preparation for reading the Psalms is the poetic quality of these texts. Hebrew poetry differs from English poetry. In English, traditional poetry is characterized by rhyme and rhythm:

> Jack and Jill
> went up the hill.

> Slowly, silently, now the moon
> Walks the night, in her silver shoon.

In Hebrew, the sense of thought determines the poetic form. Characteristic of this form is the matching of lines as parallel parts of a verse. The second line of a verse may echo or second the first. The first line makes an assertion and the second says, "Yes, and even more so this." The resulting parallelism is often memorable and comes across in English translations. Parallelism takes a variety of forms:

1. *Synonymous parallelism.* The second line enhances the thought of the first by way of a closely related statement:

> What is man that thou art mindful of him,
>> and the son of man that thou dost care for him? (Ps 8:4)

> The heavens are telling the glory of God;
>> and the firmament proclaims his handiwork. (Ps 19:1)

2. *Antithetic parallelism.* The second line may complete a thought by presenting a contrast to the first line:

> For the wicked shall be cut off;
>> but those who wait for the LORD shall possess the land. (Ps 37:9)

> For the LORD knows the way of the righteous,
>> but the way of the wicked will perish. (Ps 1:6)

3. *Stair-step parallelism.* The second line may continue the thought of the first and take it a step further:

> For the LORD is a great God,
>> and a great King above all gods. (Ps 95:3)

Students of Hebrew poetry have noticed other types of parallelism, but the above examples suffice to show that parallel lines in Hebrew poetry express nuance and completion of thought rather than entirely distinct ideas. These examples also indicate that the thought—not the sound—of the text determines its form, a form often including parallelism at various levels. Sometimes parallel lines and verses group together to form "stanzas" (Ps 119) or liturgies (Ps 95). A psalm may reflect various parts of a worship event. The sense of the psalm, though, still determines the form.

Hebrew poetry also has meter or rhythm. Many scholars have attempted to recover the basic meter, but a clear picture has not yet emerged. Some observers have argued that parallelism itself is the meter of Hebrew poetry, but there do appear to be limits to the length of a line of Hebrew poetry. Meter has not been shown to be uniform in a psalm, however, and our knowledge of the phenomenon is still limited. Thus, we need to be cautious in our discussions of meter in Hebrew poetry.[10] In any case, English translations of the Psalms seldom reflect Hebrew metrical structure. Other poetic devices such as repetition, alliteration, or assonance occur; but thought rhyme, and its parallelism, is the primary characteristic of Hebrew poetry. Awareness of this characteristic should aid in understanding the Psalms.

Conclusion

This introductory chapter has provided background for our study of the book of Psalms. Psalms are pilgrimage songs of faith and poetic compositions. The Psalter forms the primary Old Testament collection of psalms and has developed through a lengthy process. Having reviewed the basic introductory matters of the setting, shape, and poetry of the Psalter, we can now move to the exciting task of developing the best method of reading and interpreting the Psalms.

---

[10]See the discussion and bibliography in P. D. Miller, Jr., *Interpreting the Psalms* (Philadelphia: Fortress, 1986), 16–17, 29–47; other significant works include R. Alter, *The Art of Biblical Poetry* (New York: Basic Books, 1985); A. Berlin, *The Dynamics of Biblical Parallelism* (Bloomington: Indiana University, 1985). The reader should be aware that a number of interpreters now find the forms of parallelism described in this section to be outdated. The categories are, however, still helpful to students. Chapter 3 will explore this issue further.

Lessons from the Past
— 2

When we study the Bible, and especially the Psalms, we participate in a long-standing tradition. Many have taken up this worthy task, and we can learn much from those who have gone before us. For that reason, we begin our look at the ways of interpreting the Psalms by exploring the history of psalm study. This history provides significant insight into how we can better understand the Psalms.

Early Psalm Study

Much of the work on the Psalms before the twentieth century employed what might be called the personal/historical method of psalm study. If a psalm related to an individual, the central issue was authorship: Who wrote the psalm and in what circumstance in life? In the effort to answer such questions, interpreters searched for clues in psalms and their superscriptions. For example, Psalm 6 appears to be the prayer of someone suffering from an illness. Several commentators imagined a relationship between this text and Job's experience of illness and thus interpreted the prayer in light of Job's condition. Interpreters understood other psalms as prayers David spoke during particular circumstances in his life. Central was the quest for the "personal" setting out of which the psalm arose. That setting from the psalm writer's life established the framework for interpreting the text.

Other psalms did not relate to an individual but to historical events. The interpreter searched for the date and historical background of the psalm and interpreted the text in light of that background. For example, Psalms 46 and 48 describe Jerusalem under attack. Several commentators found a relationship between these texts and Sennacherib's invasion of Judah in 701 BC and thus interpreted these psalms in light of that event. Historical background and date were the keys to interpretation. The personal/historical method, then, related psalms to personal background in an individual's life or to historical background in an event in order to fully understand these texts.[1]

The primary difficulty with this approach arises from the language of the Psalms themselves. Note the examples given above. Psalm 6 could be the prayer of any person who is sick. Nothing in the psalm necessitates connecting it with Job and his illness. The general language of the text makes such an identification impossible. In like manner, Psalms 46 and 48 could refer to any attack upon Jerusalem. The identification of the historical event behind the text is in no way clear. The general language of the Psalms eventually spelled the death of the personal/historical approach in psalm scholarship.

Dating the Psalms

Early study of the Psalms concentrated on personal/historical background and on detailed study of the Hebrew text. The approach by and large remained the same until 1900; but with the dawn of the Enlightenment (an eighteenth-century movement which questioned traditional views) some of the conclusions concerning historical background changed. Many scholars began to date the Psalms late in the history of ancient Israel's religion (after 587 BC). There were several reasons for this position:

---

[1]For examples, see Hengstenberg, *Psalms*; Delitzsch, *Commentary on the Psalms*; M. Buttenwieser, *The Psalms Chronologically Treated with a New Translation* (Chicago: University of Chicago, 1938).

1. The language of the Psalms is quite eloquent, and a number of scholars held the view that such eloquence reflected late developments in the history of language. Some of the more sophisticated poetic forms in the Psalms were also judged to be late.
2. The religion of the Psalms showed an interest in priestly and liturgical issues. Again, many scholars understood the priestly aspects of ancient Israel's religion to indicate a decline in faith (a stale ritualism) and to be a late development after the high point of the pre-exilic prophets.
3. Commentators understood the superscriptions of the Psalms as later attempts to give the impression that these texts came from an earlier time.
4. Scholars understood any mention of royalty in the Psalter to relate to Maccabean princes in the second century BC.
5. Interpreters related the conflicts between enemies in the Psalms to struggles between different religious parties in post-exilic Judaism.

The late dating of the Psalms reflects assumptions about the history of language as well as the history and religion of ancient Israel that are seldom espoused today. The beginning of the twentieth century witnessed the start of a trend to date the Psalms in the time before the Babylonian exile (beginning in 587 BC), a trend that has continued until the present.[2]

Hermann Gunkel

Early psalm study narrowly focused on the personal-historical approach. The twentieth century, however, witnessed a new beginning in psalm scholarship with the work of Hermann Gunkel.[3] Gunkel regarded prior work on the Psalms as arbitrary, sentimental, and too narrowly focused. He sought a more objective, clear, and logical method. He also began to explore more fully the connection between the Psalms and worship; the as-

---

[2]For an account of this story, see R. E. Clements, *One Hundred Years of Old Testament Interpretation* (Philadelphia: Westminster, 1976), 76–98.
[3]See, for example, H. Gunkel, *The Psalms: A Form-Critical Introduction* (Facet Books, Biblical Series 19; Philadelphia: Fortress, 1967).

sumptions of many previous scholars had strangely kept them from seeing this crucial relationship.

In terms of method, Gunkel began by comparing the psalms and classifying them according to type. He perceived various types of psalms; these types had a fairly consistent form and content. Psalms of similar type or kind reflected a similar setting in ancient Israel's life. In keeping with this, Gunkel compared and classified psalms according to type. His basis for classification included the structure of the psalm, its vocabulary, and its religious tone. He listed together all hymns of praise, all petitions, and all wisdom psalms. This procedure enabled one to study all the hymns together and in comparison with other kinds of psalms. One could also study a particular hymn in light of the whole category. Such a process would construct a broader base for study. Gunkel's type-analytical method introduced a new departure in psalm interpretation; his work became foundational for contemporary psalm scholarship.

Gunkel discovered several major and minor psalm types. The major types occur more frequently in the Psalter. Gunkel's classification also affords a good introduction to the Psalter's content. Consider a description, including examples, of his categories:

1. *Hymns.* The hymns offer adoration and praise to God. Psalm 8 offers praise to the Creator; Psalm 19 praises the Creator and Lawgiver. Under this major category, Gunkel listed three sub-types and their distinguishing characteristics:

   Songs of Zion. These hymns praise God as the one who is present with the community of faith in Zion (Jerusalem). Psalms 46 and 48 show God protecting the city of Zion and its people. Psalm 122 offers praise to Yahweh during pilgrimage to Zion for worship.

   Enthronement Psalms. These hymns celebrate the kingship of God. Psalm 47 celebrates God's sovereign kingship over all the earth. Psalm 93 describes God's rule over the chaotic powers that bring disorder to the earth.

   Old Testament Hymns Outside the Psalter. We noted a number of these earlier. Exodus 15:1–18 celebrates God's deliverance of the people from the Egyptians at the "Reed

Sea." First Samuel 2:1–10 celebrates God's answering Hannah's prayer for a child.

2. *Community Laments.* A lament is a prayer for help in the midst of crisis. Ancient Israel often found itself in a crisis affecting the whole community, such as a military crisis or a harvest disaster or plague and pestilence. The community faces military defeat in Psalm 44; wicked enemies pose the threat in Psalm 58. In such settings, the community prayed for help.

3. *Individual Laments.* Individuals within the community also prayed for help. The speaker in Psalm 3 is in trouble and surrounded by enemies. Psalm 6 is a prayer for healing from sickness. The Psalter contains numerous individual laments. Gunkel understood these psalms to reflect autobiographical settings, but he thought that the texts had been shaped to facilitate their use by various people in similar crises. The Psalms reflect real individual crises, though a precise identification of the problem is often difficult. The enemies, often mentioned in these psalms, are also difficult to identify. Gunkel noticed also that these honest prayers in the midst of crisis affirm that God hears the prayer. The texts often conclude in a positive way, expressing certainty that God hears the prayer, or pledging to give praise to the God who delivers; the speaker may even offer enthusiastic praise to God. Gunkel listed one sub-type under this category:

Psalms of Trust. In these texts, the expression of trust often found in the laments has been expanded into a complete psalm. Psalm 11 expresses trust in the midst of overwhelming disorder. The first part of Psalm 27 affirms trust in God even in the face of many enemies.

4. *Individual Psalms of Thanksgiving.* Just as persons in the community of ancient Israel prayed for help, they also gave thanks to God for that help when it arrived. Such is the case in the psalms of thanksgiving. An individual prayed for help in the midst of trouble and God delivered. These psalms express, as a part of worship, the person's thanksgiving for that deliverance. It was perhaps done as a fulfillment of a vow of praise like those found in the lament psalms. Psalm 30 gives thanks for deliverance from the grip of death. Psalm 32 offers thanksgiving for deliverance from the power of sin.

5. *Royal Psalms.* Royal psalms relate to the king in Jerusalem. They refer to the whole line of Davidic kings as well as the current occupant of the throne. The king served as political and military leader of ancient Israel, but he was also the leader of worship and the channel of blessing/cursing from God. The blessing was dependent on the king's righteousness. The king had a special relationship with Yahweh and was the Lord's representative in ruling over the people. The king also represented the people in prayer to Yahweh. Because of this background, the royal psalms constituted a major category for Gunkel, even though such psalms are few in number. These psalms relate to special occasions in the religious services for the king. Psalm 2 relates to the king's coronation and describes the king as God's "adopted" son. Psalm 20 is a prayer for the king as he prepares to go into battle.

In addition to these major types, Gunkel also listed seven distinctive minor types.

1. *Pilgrimage Songs.* Pilgrims sang these psalms while journeying to worship in the temple. These texts are related to the Songs of Zion mentioned above.
2. *Community Psalms of Thanksgiving.* Just as there are individual psalms of thanksgiving, the Psalter also contains texts in which the community offers thanks for deliverance from a crisis facing the whole nation: war, famine, epidemic, etc. Psalm 67 probably reflects some type of harvest disaster; Psalm 124 celebrates deliverance from the enemy.
3. *Wisdom Psalms.* These texts relate to other Old Testament wisdom material, such as Proverbs, Job, and Ecclesiastes. The perspective of the wisdom psalms is often reminiscent of Proverbs. These psalms provide wise instruction for daily living, guidance for living a full life. Psalm 1 describes the life of the righteous, in contrast to the wicked, as prosperous. Psalm 49 asserts that those who are confident in their undeserved wealth will enjoy only brief prosperity.
4. *General Liturgies.* Gunkel identified three types of liturgies or texts in which there is a change of speaker. General liturgies contain a variety of elements. Psalm 60 includes lament, petition, and a word from God, as well as further lament and an expression of confidence. Psalm 82 reflects a change of voice, with God speaking in the council of the gods.

5. *Prophetic Liturgies.* These liturgies contain a prophetic warning spoken by the worship leader and are usually put in the form of an oracle, a word from God, calling the people to faithfulness. Psalm 95 begins with a double call to worship but concludes with a warning calling the community to obedience. Psalm 126 begins with thanksgiving and lament and then urges confidence.

6. *"Torah" Liturgies.* In these liturgies, pilgrims approach the place of worship and ask who is qualified to enter. The priest then gives instruction or "torah" on that subject, and the faithful enter to worship. Psalm 15, a "torah" or entrance song, reflects just such a structure. Psalm 24 begins with praise, moves through an entrance liturgy, and with God's entrance concludes in worship.

7. *Mixed Types.* Gunkel argued that some psalms contain elements of various literary types, and thus he placed them in a separate category of mixed types. Psalm 9–10 (originally one composition) is both thanksgiving and lament. Psalm 36 relates to the categories of lament, hymn, and wisdom.

Gunkel's classification is a good starting point for studying the Psalms. Psalms scholars today follow Gunkel's lead and begin with classification. Classifications vary, but most would agree that the Psalter includes hymns and laments as well as individual and community psalms. An emphasis on the royal psalms has also continued. Gunkel's enumeration of the psalm types, then, has made a lasting contribution. Also worthy of note is his method of comparison in order to achieve the classification.

The other issue that Gunkel addressed was the setting in ancient Israel's life from which the various psalm types derived. Gunkel took the view that the various types of psalms originated in worship. The psalms in the Psalter imitate those types but were written at a time when psalms were no longer used in the original worship setting. Many today would question this latter point, but Gunkel's search for the original setting of the Psalms and his discussion of their relation to worship are still noteworthy.

Gunkel was a product of his time. He still dated the Psalms rather late in the history of ancient Israel's religion, in part because of his bias against "priestly" religion. The limitations of Gunkel's work, however, do not diminish his achievement. He brought renewed excitement and emphasis to the study of the Psalms; he has left an influential legacy. R. E. Clements comments:

> The greatness of Gunkel's achievement in pioneering a new ap-
> proach to the Psalms and thereby opening up new possibilities
> of understanding them in relation to Israel's worship and spir-
> ituality remains unchallenged. A whole new era of psalm studies
> became possible on the basis of the classification of psalm types
> and the related lines of interpretation which he established. Not
> only so but he had also shown up very clearly the unsatis-
> factoriness of a number of false trails which had for long been
> followed by psalm commentators.[4]

Gunkel emphasized the types of psalms and their origin in worship, and his work has influenced most contemporary inter-preters of the Psalms. On pages 22 and 23 is a working classi-fication of the Psalms. This classification certainly reflects Gunkel's influence and is essentially self-explanatory; however, two com-ments are in order. First, the classification also reflects the influ-ence of Claus Westermann.[5] He has argued convincingly that the major division in the Psalms is between praise and lament. He has also shown that hymns and thanksgiving psalms reflect two ways of performing the same activity: offering praise to God. Thus I have placed the thanksgiving psalms in the praise category. I have likewise included the trust psalms in the praise category be-cause of their hymnic quality.

Classifying the Psalms according to type helps organize our study of the book. Reading the Psalter from Psalm 1 through Psalm 150 is confusing. Organizing one's reading according to the psalm types is a more helpful procedure. We then can study the Zion psalms together and the royal psalms together and the com-munity thanksgiving psalms together and the community laments together, and so forth. This classification of the Psalms will be foundational for everything else we do.

---

[4]Clements, *One Hundred Years*, 82.
[5]See C. Westermann, *Praise and Lament in the Psalms* (Atlanta: John Knox, 1981).

A CLASSIFICATION OF THE PSALMS

I. Praise

A. General Hymns
    29, 33, 68, 100, 103, 105, 111, 113, 114, 115, 117, 134, 135, 139, 145, 146, 147, 149, 150

B. Creation Psalms
    8, 19, 65, 104, 148

C. Enthronement Psalms   *Kingship*
    47, 93, 95, 96, 97, 98, 99

D. Zion Psalms
    46, 48, 76, 84, 87, 122

E. Entrance Liturgies
    15, 24

F. Hymns with Prophetic Warnings
    50, 81, 82

G. Trust Psalms
    23, 91, 121, 125, 131

H. Thanksgiving Psalms

    1. Individual Psalms
       30, 34, 41, 66, 92, 116, 118, 138

    2. Community Psalms
       67, 75, 107, 124, 129, 136

II. Lament

A. Individual Psalms
    3, 4, 5, 6, 7, 9–10, 11, 13, 16, 17, 22, 25, 26, 27, 28, 31, 35, 36, 38, 39, 40, 42–43, 51, 52, 54, 55, 56, 57, 59, 61, 62, 63, 64, 69, 70, 71, 77, 86, 88, 94, 102, 109, 120, 130, 140, 141, 142, 143

B. Community Psalms
    12, 14, 44, 53, 58, 60, 74, 79, 80, 83, 85, 90, 106, 108, 123, 126, 137

III. Royal Psalms
2, 18, 20, 21, 45, 72, 89, 101, 110, 132, 144

IV. Wisdom Psalms
1, 32, 37, 49, 73, 78, 112, 119, 127, 128, 133

Gunkel's emphasis on the psalm types and their relation to worship is a good place to begin in interpreting the Psalms. It also gives us the first question to ask when interpreting a particular psalm: *What are the type and structure of the psalm?* We will pursue this question further in chapter 4.

Sigmund Mowinckel

Gunkel had argued that the psalm types originated in ancient Israel's worship. Gunkel's student, Sigmund Mowinckel,[6] argued not only that the psalm types originated in worship but that most of the psalms in our Psalter were also used as a part of worship. The Psalms speak of performing worship activities, and Mowinckel understood such references not as "poetic fiction" but as reality. The Psalms were a part of ancient Israel's living worship, and Mowinckel sought to understand their background in worship. Gunkel analyzed the types of psalms; Mowinckel took his teacher's work to its logical conclusion by analyzing the use of psalms in worship. He felt that personal religion and the religion of corporate worship are not mutually exclusive but are one and the same. A psalm used in corporate worship could have great spiritual impact. Thus Mowinckel saw the task of psalm interpretation as primarily an investigation into the setting of the Psalms, and he sought that setting in ancient Israel's worship. Questions for Mowinckel would include: In what festival was a particular hymn used? From what kind of ritual did a prayer for help derive? How did the psalm function in ancient Israel's worship?

Mowinckel's method could be called "cult-functional." The word "cult" necessitates a brief comment. The word signifies organized worship. It does not indicate some aberrant expression of faith or abnormal behavior; cult is rather a technical term indicating primarily, though not exclusively, the organized

---

[6]See S. Mowinckel, *The Psalms in Israel's Worship* (2 vols.; Nashville: Abingdon, 1962).

worship of ancient Israel in the temple. Accordingly, Mowinckel sought to discover how psalms functioned in this context. He understood worship (cult) to have a primary place in Old Testament religion. Other elements included belief (doctrine) and ethics (behavior), but worship helped the congregation understand doctrine and gave impetus to ethical living. Consequently, Mowinckel held the cult to be central to ancient Israel's faith and its understanding indispensable for interpreting the Psalms.

Mowinckel went further in describing ancient Israel's worship. He understood worship to be the visible and audible expression of the relationship between congregation and deity. This definition makes it clear that Mowinckel presumed worship to be a dramatic event. Worship included both sights and sounds: There were processionals, elaborate rituals (including dances), and offerings; furthermore, worshipers bowed or prostrated themselves before God in worship. Worship would have included speaking, expressing joy, and singing. The Old Testament pictures ancient Israel's worship as carefully orchestrated and as having great dramatic effect.

Ancient Israel's worship, in Mowinckel's view, also related to the community's own faith history. The people shared a faith tradition, and in worship they remembered that tradition; they remembered it through its dramatic reenactment in worship. As a result, the worshiping congregation could see the impact of the great events of their people's faith history; they could in a dramatic way participate in the story of their faith. The result was a congregation renewed for faithful living. For example, the exodus from Egypt would be represented dramatically, and the current congregation could understand that God, in the same way, delivers them from oppression. Deuteronomy 6:20–26 also illustrates this point. In that passage one generation narrates the exodus story to another generation with the use of first person plural pronouns: "the LORD brought *us* out of Egypt" (v. 21). Mowinckel viewed this remembering of ancient Israel's faith traditions as the primary reason for the cult's existence. This perspective also reveals why drama is so important for Mowinckel.

Mowinckel was influenced by comparative ancient Near Eastern texts and by anthropological studies on "primitive" religions in the ancient world. Some have criticized his use of such materials, and it may have colored his work on occasion, but his work still has had a lasting impact on our comprehension of the Psalms. Comment on several psalms will illustrate the value of Mowinckel's work.

Psalm 26 is a lament in which the worshiper speaks of going around the altar in the sanctuary while singing thanksgiving to God. The speaker declares personal innocence with a symbolic washing of the hands. Psalm 5 describes the preparation of a sacrifice and the worshiper's waiting for its effect. The text also warns that the wicked person is not allowed into the life-renewing cult, while the righteous worshiper is. Psalm 100 speaks of entering the temple while singing praise to God. Psalm 95 apparently began in the temple court with a call to worship the Creator. The people, singing, then went into the sanctuary and were again called to worship and bow down to God their redeemer. The psalm concludes with a prophetic warning against faithlessness. These psalms show particular actions in worship as Mowinckel described it.

Mowinckel's primary contribution to psalm study, then, centers on the relationship between psalm and cult. The Psalms originated in the cult and thus were closely related to the temple and its personnel. Mowinckel concentrated on the pre-exilic cult in Jerusalem. This indicates that he thought most of the Psalms came from the pre-exilic period. His position continued the trend toward an earlier dating of these texts. Gunkel had actually made some initial moves in that direction. Mowinckel also made specific proposals about worship settings reflected in the Psalms; we will return to those proposals in later chapters. At this point, however, we need to note the more fundamental point of the relation between the Psalms and worship. Mowinckel argued that the Psalms originated and were used in the cult. Gunkel concentrated on psalm types and structures; Mowinckel emphasized the use of psalms in ancient Israel's cult. Mowinckel has provided us with a second question to ask when interpreting a psalm: *How was this psalm used in worship?*

Recent Studies

This chapter explores the questions essential for interpreting the book of Psalms, the hymnbook of the Bible. We have
looked at questions of type/structure and use in worship. If we
were to stop at this point, we would run the risk of being limited
to an ancient past; much of the discussion thus far has related
to questions of origin. The work of Gunkel and Mowinckel is
foundational and is the basis for most twentieth-century studies
of the Psalms, but their methods leave many unanswered questions. What happened to the Psalms after their origin and setting disappeared? How were the Psalms understood when the
Jerusalem cult no longer functioned? How did the Psalms come
together as a book? A number of recent studies have discussed
these issues.[7] These questions prod us forward in our search for
the best way to interpret the Psalms.

Perhaps the most prominent scholar asking questions like
those above is Brevard Childs. Childs has linked the process of
interpretation closely with the Bible's canonical context. After the
texts originated, they moved toward inclusion in the Hebrew
canon. Childs has described some ways in which the community
shaped these texts into the canonical book of Psalms. Human
words in response to God have now become part of God's Word
and instruction to persons. Some have found Childs's emphasis
on canon to be problematic; nonetheless, he has raised unavoid-
able questions about what has happened to psalms between the
time of their origin and of their inclusion in the Old Testament
book of Psalms. Two issues are central: (1) How did the believing
community shape psalms according to its needs? (2) How did the
Psalter come together as a collection? Both questions relate to the
redaction, or editing, of the Psalms. We can note several concerns
that were operative.

---

[7]See, for example, Westermann, *Praise and Lament*, 250–58;
Childs, *Introduction*, 504–25; G. H. Wilson, *The Editing of the Hebrew Psalter*
(SBLDS 76; Chico: Scholars, 1985); Miller, *Interpreting*, 11–15.

Community Emphasis

Many psalms relate to the life of the individual, but there is evidence that later generations applied these texts to the experience of the community. Psalm 130 is the prayer of an individual, but it ends with a word of hope for the community:

> O Israel, hope in the LORD!
>   For with the LORD there is steadfast love,
>   and with him is plenteous redemption.
> And he will redeem Israel
>   from all his iniquities. (vv. 7, 8)

Psalm 25 exhibits the same feature. The community, through its leaders, reinterpreted and redacted psalms in light of its needs.

Influence from the Exile

Childs has noted the view that ancient Israel reinterpreted psalms in light of the experience of the Babylonian exile. The exile was a major trauma for the community, and songs of faith were shaped in relation to needs coming out of that experience. Psalm 22 is an individual lament; but its conclusion may derive from the experience of exile, thus applying this individual prayer on suffering to the experience of the whole community during exile. A similar concern may be operative in Psalm 9–10. The community shaped psalms in relation to its changing needs, some of which emerged from the crisis of exile.

Hope for the Future

Related to influences from the exile is a prominent emphasis on hope for the future. Yahweh will intervene in the future to bring glory to the people. The conclusion of Psalm 69 shows this emphasis. In addition, the lament psalms consistently move from sorrow in the present to hope for the future. The initial readers of the Psalms stood in a setting in which they hoped for the yet-to-be-seen kingdom of God. Psalm 102 speaks both of lament and a future hope.

The royal psalms are also worthy of note at this point. These psalms initially referred to the Davidic line in Jerusalem;

but by the time of the completion of the book of Psalms, there was no king in Jerusalem. The community had come to understand the royal psalms as messianic psalms bearing witness to hope for the messianic kingdom.

The Language of the Psalter

The general, even vague, nature of psalm language was noted earlier. Such language is part of the reason that the import of the Psalms has endured through the centuries. The language is universally applicable and adaptable. It is adaptable for life and open to use by many. This feature is also part of the reason behind ancient Israel's reinterpretation of these texts. This kind of language makes possible the application of these texts to a community no longer tied to the pre-exilic Jerusalem cult. Clues of original cultic settings are still present, but the language is also now open to a broader interpretation as Scripture for the life of faith. The recurrence of some psalms shows that their language can be reinterpreted for different settings. Compare Psalm 14 with Psalm 53 or Psalm 108 with Psalms 57:7–11 and 60:6–12. Psalms 112 and 119 also reflect the concern to relate the Psalter to a pilgrimage of faith that is not tied to the Jerusalem cult. This "universalizing" of psalm language is part of the community's reinterpretation of the Psalms after the demise of the temple cult.

Superscriptions

Chapter 1 noted the importance of the psalm superscriptions. They include a number of cultic terms, but they also emphasize the relation between David and the Psalms. Several superscriptions include historical incidents from David's life. These notes picture David not as glorious king but as a representative person engaged in the life of faith. Such an interpretation of a psalm helps readers envision the text's impact in a particular setting. Then readers can see how the psalm might function in similar settings in their own lives. The reading of the Psalms reflected in the superscriptions helps the believing community reapply these texts as pilgrimage songs of faith.

The Organization of the Psalter

We have already noted the intentional shaping, over time, of the Psalter as a collection of psalms. This process completed the reinterpretation/redaction of the Psalms. Psalm 1 introduces the book by making it clear that the Psalter is to be seen as instruction ("torah" in v. 2) for righteous living. The book concentrates on an essential aspect of the life of faith and righteousness: prayer, the dialogue that nourishes a relationship with God. The conclusion of the book (Ps 150) calls for a symphony of praise, indicating that the life of righteousness has been worth the effort. The Psalter also reflects the move from individual and lament psalms, dominant in the first part of the book, to community and praise psalms, in the latter part of the book. The organization of the Psalter thus also reflects the process of reinterpretation and redaction. The configuration of the book affords a context for interpreting individual psalms.

The presence of these concerns in the Psalms indicates that the community shaped the Psalter in accordance with the life of faith. The community redacted some psalms: Psalm 51 concludes with a section that no doubt comes from a later editor and applies that text to the community in the time after the destruction of Jerusalem in 587 BC. The community also shaped the book of Psalms as a whole. How a psalm fits into the context of the book is important in interpretation. Psalm 100 is a general hymn of praise, but it concludes a collection of psalms celebrating God's kingship and precedes a royal psalm. Observations like these can enhance the task of interpretation.

Summary

These recent studies have presented a variety of issues in psalm study; most, however, relate to the redaction or reinterpretation of the Psalms. Perhaps we could label the whole process "shaping." The community has shaped psalms in relation to its life, and it has shaped the book of Psalms as its normative collection of songs of faith. Both parts of the process are implied in the third question to be asked when interpreting a psalm: *How has the community shaped the psalm?*

Conclusion

This chapter has explored the history of psalm study as a means of discovering the major questions to ask when studying the Psalms. The works of Gunkel, Mowinckel, and Childs (along with others) have raised three issues: type/structure, use in worship, and reinterpretation/redaction. When beginning to study a psalm, considering these issues and reading in the material suggested in the bibliography on page 151 can greatly enhance the study of the text. Some brief examples might help show the significance of this strategy.

Psalm 6 is a lament—as are Psalms 3–5 and 7—which follows the usual pattern of an individual lament. We will consider that structure in chapter 4. The psalm is probably a prayer of someone who is quite ill (vv. 2, 5–7); as a result, it may have been used in a ritual of prayer for divine healing. The psalm contains language, however, that can be interpreted figuratively and thus applied to any major crisis. Verses 8–10 indicate that the one who prays the psalm stands between the crisis and the fulfillment of a divine promise of healing. These observations about Psalm 6 in response to the three questions raised above give the interpreter of the psalm a tremendous step towards applying the psalm to the life of faith.

Psalm 100 is a general hymn of praise following the typical hymnic patterns that are discussed in chapter 5. The psalm was used in a service, perhaps a festival, of praise that included a procession into the temple, accompanied by the singing of praise to Yahweh (vv. 2, 4). Sometimes that kind of observation is all we can say about a psalm's use in worship, though reading in a good study Bible or commentary may give additional information. Even so, attention to the role of the psalm in worship reminds the reader that the text is not just a general affirmation about God; rather, it reflects God's involvement in a worship event in history. Such a perspective opens the possibility of the same experience for the contemporary worshiping community. The praise in Psalm 100 is quite general. The superscription relates the psalm to "the thank offering," perhaps offered in gratitude for God's faithfulness toward the people (v. 5). We have noted above, however, that the psalm concludes the collection of psalms on the kingship of God and immediately precedes a royal psalm. In its context in the Psalter, then, Psalm 100 can be interpreted as praise and thanksgiving for God's faithful kingship. Our interpretive questions have again contributed substantial insight as we begin to interpret this text.

Psalm 101 affords a final example. This text is a royal psalm and a pledge by the king to preserve justice in the land. The king would be in such a position of authority (vv. 5, 6, 8) and would rule over the royal house (v. 7). The psalm is a kind of "oath of office" and thus may well have been a part of the coronation ceremony, or the anniversary of that ceremony, for the Davidic king. By the time of the completion of the Psalter, the text no doubt related to the messianic age and its ushering in of justice. The psalm is also capable of a broader interpretation, calling upon the worshiping community to bring about justice in life. These comments fix a point of departure for understanding the psalm.

These examples indicate that the three interpretive questions we have noted do provide a significant beginning for interpreting the Psalms. Before taking the next step in studying the Psalms, let us conclude this chapter by listing the questions we have discussed:

1. What is the type/structure of the psalm?
2. How was the psalm used in worship?
3. How has the community shaped the psalm?

Reading the Psalms

3

The last chapter concentrated on how the history of psalm scholarship could help in developing questions to ask when studying the Psalms. Concerns about type/structure, cultic function, and shaping surfaced. Attention to these matters helps identify the context out of which the Psalms came and thus provides guidelines for the interpreter. One might otherwise simply read the Psalms according to personal whims. In addition to context, the other guide for the interpreter is, of course, the text itself. Our approach in chapter 2 was deductive from the history of psalm scholarship; however, reading psalms inductively is precisely what has brought scholars to the interpretive issues we have explored. When students begin to read the Psalms, they notice similarities and differences in the kinds of structures in the texts and begin to wonder how to organize their study. Such were the concerns of Gunkel. Readers also notice references to worship—altar, feasts, entering Yahweh's presence, the congregation—and wonder about their origin, also Mowinckel's concern. Readers who ask questions about where these texts came from might also want to know what happened to them later and how they were organized into the book of Psalms—the matter of shaping. These questions continue to confront those who study the Psalms in any detail.

A number of recent works in Old Testament scholarship have encouraged greater intentionality in the careful reading of texts like the Psalms. These studies have focused on literary features of texts, which are regarded as clues to a psalm's interpretation. This type of literary approach can build on previous scholarship and helps us make the next step in our search for the best ways to interpret the Psalms.

Literary Study of the Psalter

> It is simply the fact that as soon as we perceive that a verbal sequence has a sustained rhythm, that it is formally structured according to a continuously operating principle of organization, we know that we are in the presence of poetry and we respond to it accordingly.[1]

We have already identified the Psalms as poetry. Poetry is a succinct, highly structured means of expression. "These ancient makers of devotional and celebratory poems were keenly aware that poetry is the most complex ordering of language, and perhaps also the most demanding."[2] The poetry of the Psalter exploits Hebrew literary conventions in order to involve the reader in the Psalms' drama. As noted earlier, the Psalms contain many common threads. The Hebrew poetic tradition exerted powerful influence over its writers.[3] Nonetheless, the careful reader can appreciate the great variety of poetic skill in these psalms.

The first chapter mentioned several recent studies on Hebrew poetry.[4] A number of these studies have concentrated on parallelism. Our study has described parallelism as a kind of echo effect intrinsic to Hebrew poetry. Others would argue that this effect defies such a simple description. At the least, Hebrew poetry exhibits parallel structures on a variety of levels—matching

---

[1]B. H. Smith, *Poetic Closure: A Study of How Poems End* (Chicago: University of Chicago Press, 1970), 23.

[2]Alter, *Art of Biblical Poetry*, 136.

[3]See ibid., 190: "Stock imagery, as I have intimated, is the staple of biblical poetry, and Psalms is the preeminent instance of its repeated deployment."

[4]See note 10 in chapter 1.

words, phrases, lines, and thought sequences. Our purpose is
not to describe the various types of parallelism, but to alert the
reader to the phenomenon and to say that attention to parallel
structures can enliven one's encounter with a psalm.[5]

A number of recent works also point to additional literary
features of the poetry of the Psalter: repetition, word play, am-
biguity, figures of speech. Considering such features can help us
understand a text and partake of the feel of a powerful psalm.
Robert Alter has noted the deceptive simplicity of psalms; they
seem so simple and yet often exhibit an artistic structure with profound meaning.[6]

> The Psalms are of course poems written out of deep and often
> passionate faith. What I am proposing is that the poetic medium
> made it possible to articulate the emotional freight, the moral
> consequences, the altered perception of the world that flowed
> from this monotheistic belief, in compact verbal structures that
> could in some instances seem simplicity itself. Psalms, at least
> in the guise of cultic hymns, were a common poetic genre
> throughout the ancient Near East, but as the form was adopted
> by Hebrew poets, it often became an instrument for expressing
> in a collective voice (whether first person plural or singular) a
> distinctive, sometimes radically new, sense of time, space, history,
> creation, and the character of individual destiny. In keeping with
> this complex expressive purpose, many psalms, on scrutiny,
> prove to have a finely tensile semantic weave that one would
> not expect from the seeming conventionality of the language.[7]

The poems grow in specificity and intensity. Alter suggests that
close attention to the literary features of texts enables the interpreter to "enter the world of the text" and gain a fuller appre-
ciation for it.

---

[5]For the various dimensions of parallelism, see especially J. L.
Kugel, *The Idea of Biblical Poetry: Parallelism and Its History* (New Haven:
Yale University Press, 1981); Alter, *Art of Biblical Poetry,* 3–26; Miller, *Inter-
preting,* 16–17, 29–47; Berlin, *Dynamics of Parallelism.*

[6]See Alter, *Art of Biblical Poetry,* 111–36; idem, "Psalms," *The
Literary Guide to the Bible,* ed. R. Alter and F. Kermode (Cambridge, Mass.:
Harvard University Press, 1987), 251–55.

[7]Ibid., 113–14.

Walter Brueggemann's work on the Psalter has also emphasized the Psalms' use of language.[8] His treatment does not concentrate on the details of Hebrew poetry as much as on the literary techniques psalms depend upon to communicate their message. Careful consideration of a psalm's use of language and literary techniques has enabled Brueggemann to locate the central turning point of texts and thus discover the primary import of psalms.

Other, briefer studies have demonstrated the value of rhetorical analysis for the interpretation of various psalms.[9] The Psalms use language to evoke a response in the hearer/reader. This function of language is called rhetoric, and a number of Old Testament scholars now suggest that psalm study should include a treatment of rhetoric, how a psalm uses language to communicate persuasively its message.

When examining a psalm, take notice of its rhetoric. Begin this process by asking about the purpose of the psalm. Interpreters of narrative passages often note the importance of understanding a story's plot. The plot may center on a conflict that seeks resolution. In a sense, psalms also have a plot, or at least a central goal. The reader can often discover the central purpose of the poem from its opening lines; it begins with either a plea or a call to praise. A plea seeks resolution of a crisis, and a call to praise seeks response from the addressee. Other psalms relate to a task, such as establishing justice or living faithfully. Many psalms conclude in an open-ended way with a renewed call to the addressee concerning the purpose at hand. The text then moves from this main goal toward some type of denouement.

---

[8]See W. Brueggemann, *Praying the Psalms* (Winona, Minn.: Saint Mary's Press, 1982); idem, *The Message of the Psalms: A Theological Commentary* (Minneapolis: Augsburg, 1984).

[9]P. G. Mosca, "Psalm 26: Poetic Structure and the Form-Critical Task," *CBQ* 47 (1985): 212–37; G. S. Ogden, "Psalm 60: Its Rhetoric, Form, and Function," *JSOT* 31 (1985): 83–94; L. C. Allen, "The Value of Rhetorical Criticism in Psalm 69," *JBL* 105 (1986): 577–98. See also W. H. Bellinger, Jr., "Let the Words of My Mouth: Proclaiming the Psalms," *Southwestern Journal of Theology* 27 (1984): 17–24.

Biblical poetry, as I have tried to show, is characterized by an intensifying or narrative development within the line; and quite often this "horizontal" movement is then projected downward in a "vertical" focusing movement through a sequence of lines or even through a whole poem. What this means is that the poetry of the Bible is concerned above all with dynamic process moving toward some culmination.[10]

An awareness of movement in a psalm can furnish a framework for examining how the text uses language to achieve its goal. Within that framework, four questions construct a foundation for studying the text's language. The student can answer these questions simply by reading a good translation of the psalm. Knowledge of the original Hebrew of the Psalms would enrich the study, but it is not mandatory. A translation that is consistent in its renderings will suffice. Attention to these questions may lead to an even closer reading of a psalm and enable the reader to notice other features of the text's language. Here are the four questions for an initial examination of a psalm's rhetoric:

1. How does the psalm use divine names?
2. What words or phrases (or synonyms) does the psalm repeat?
3. How does the text use "loaded" terms such as "justice, righteousness, steadfast love?" Loaded terms carry special significance for the tradition of ancient Israel's faith.
4. What figures of speech (metaphors, images) does the psalm incorporate?

Asking these questions of a psalm can help with the task of interpretation.

This brief discussion of literary studies in the Psalter would suggest two tasks for the careful reader of the Psalms. *First*, note the parallel structures in the text. How does the psalm use echo effects? *Second*, with the aid of the four questions above, describe the "plot" of the poem. Some illustrations will demonstrate the value of these procedures.

---

[10] Alter, *The Literary Guide*, 620.

Examples

Psalm 103 uses a variety of parallel structures. It begins with three instances of the word "bless" and then moves to five phrases with the word "who." The psalm is a response to God as the one who gives life. Note the verbs: God forgives, heals, redeems, crowns, satisfies, works. Verse 6 begins with "The LORD" and continues to speak of Yahweh's work as the basis of praise. The revelation of God's works becomes more specific in v. 7 with Moses and the people of Israel. Verses 9 and 10 contain four negative phrases; God does not give persons what they deserve but is more generous. Verses 11–14 continue the psalm's line of thought with an interesting literary pattern. Verses 11 and 14 give reasons for God's gracious generosity: steadfast love and the recognition that without God's help, humans are but dust. Verses 12 and 13 then use comparisons to describe God's mercy:

> as far as the east is from the west,
> so far does he remove our transgressions from us.
> As a father pities his children,
> so the LORD pities those who fear him.

Note the parallelism in the two verses. In addition, vv. 11 and 14 begin (in Hebrew) one way, and vv. 12 and 13 begin another. We might then call the pattern of these verses AB B'A'. The next section, vv. 15–18, emphasizes a contrast that has informed the entire text: the contrast between the ways of Yahweh and the ways of human beings. Note the use of loaded terms in this section: "steadfast love" (four times in the psalm), "mercy" (also in v. 8), "justice, vindication, righteousness, covenant." Verses 15–18 also draw upon a vivid image to describe the central contrast of the psalm. In contrast to the fading grass, God is reliable. The psalm then appropriately concludes with four uses of "bless."

The instances of "bless" in the last verses of the psalm remind us of the beginning of the text. The psalm begins and ends with the same pattern. The technique of setting off a piece of literature by repetition is common in the Old Testament.[11] Both the beginning (vv. 1–5) and ending (vv. 19–22) of the psalm emphasize response to God: "Bless the LORD, O my soul!" The middle sections of the text (vv. 6–14 and vv. 15–18) emphasize the contrast between God and humanity. So the pattern of the psalm, in line with vv. 11–14, is AB B′A′. Utilizing comparison and contrast, the psalm produces an artful composition that powerfully praises and asserts God's constancy. Verse 8 summarizes this proclamation by way of synonymous parallelism in terms characteristic of the Old Testament:

> The LORD is merciful and gracious,
> slow to anger and abounding in steadfast love.

Such an analysis of Psalm 103 gives the reader valuable information for the interpretive task.

Additional examples may help illustrate the method of rhetorical analysis. The lament psalms often exhibit powerful language; *Psalm 13* is characteristic of this psalm type. The text begins with four uses of "how long?" Pay heed to the parallel lines. In vv. 3 and 4, the worshiper asks for help; note the verbs: "consider, answer, lighten." The presence of the divine name is also noteworthy in this psalm. "Yahweh" is used in vv. 1, 3, and 6. Verse 3 contains an intimate form of address: "O LORD my God." Verses 3 and 4 also provide motivation for divine answer to the prayer with the fourfold repetition, "lest, lest, lest, lest" (the worshiper die). Then the reader waits; the turning point of the psalm comes after v. 4. The last two verses begin with "But I . . . " and show a correspondence between the rejoicing of the subjects, "I, myself, I," and the dealings of Yahweh, "thy (salvation), thy (steadfast love)." Yahweh has answered the plea; the conflict is resolved.

---

[11]Ibid., 255–56, notes the frequency of this "envelope structure." Smith, *Poetic Closure*, 92, suggests that the change from three to four uses of "bless" is a typical sign of poetic closure.

Psalm 86 illustrates further literary techniques used in psalms.[12] Verses 1-4, 6, 16, and 17 contain petitions (incline, preserve, save, be gracious, gladden, take pity); vv. 13 and 17 hint at the divine answer. The psalm is a powerful prayer addressed to the God of "steadfast love" (vv. 5, 13, 15). This perspective is confirmed by the presence of the second person pronoun, the emphasis on God's uniqueness (vv. 8, 10), and the occurrence of traditional terms of ancient Israel's faith that appear in the doxologies of vv. 5, 10, and 15, all of which construct a kind of stair-step parallelism. The relational aspect of the psalm becomes apparent when the reader notices descriptions of the worshiper (vv. 2, 3, 4, 16) that correspond to the descriptions of God. The worshiper seeks Yahweh's help, as do others who identify with the speaker. These comments on Psalms 13 and 86 only briefly illustrate the laments' vivid language.

Psalm 1 also provides an interesting text for rhetorical analysis. Contrasting images of the moral categories of righteous and wicked dominate the psalm. The text compares the blessed and obedient person to the luxuriant tree (vv. 1-3), the wicked to the chaff that disappears (v. 4). The consequences of life's choices are unequivocal. Such a perspective fits well a wisdom psalm seeking to nurture faith. The final verse emphasizes the message with antithetic parallelism:

> for the LORD knows the way of the righteous,
> but the way of the wicked will perish.

Note the presence of the divine name in the last verse; its only other occurrence is in verse 2, in the phrase "the law of the LORD." The verbs of the first verse—"walks, stands, sits"—confirm that the psalm is about lifestyle. The repetition of "wicked" (and synonyms "sinners, scoffers") and "righteous," also important terms in the Old Testament faith tradition, verifies the didactic lesson of the psalm: choose the righteous life. These brief

---

[12]See Brueggemann's treatment of this psalm, *Message of the Psalms*, 60–63.

comments on Psalm 1 afford the reader beneficial insight for the task of interpretation.

Psalm 101 is a final example. The only occurrences of the divine name are in the first and last verses. The opening of the psalm makes clear that this text is a promise sung to Yahweh, and the frequent repetition of "I will" corroborates the promissory character of the text. The psalm betrays an intimate relationship between the speaker and the recipient of the vow (Yahweh). The verbs ("walk, practices") indicate that the text is about the speaker's lifestyle; the psalm centers on the life of the speaker with the use of first person singular pronouns. Strong terms also paint the contrast between justice ("loyalty, justice, blameless, integrity") and evil ("perverseness, evil, deceit, wicked"). Consistently making use of synonymous parallelism, Psalm 101 is a powerful oath to produce justice in the life of the speaker and of the community. Even this cursory look at the psalm's use of language is valuable for the interpretive process.

These illustrations demonstrate the rich language of the Psalms. Attention to this feature can render precious interpretive clues for the reader and help the reader enter the literary world of the text. Considering the function of parallelism, divine names, repetition, traditional terms from ancient Israel's faith, and figures of speech affords a beginning point in a rhetorical analysis of psalms. These rhetorical techniques are all part of a fourth question to ask when studying a psalm: *How does the psalm use language?*

Conclusion

We have begun to focus on the texts within the book of Psalms; the texts function as pilgrimage songs of faith for the worshiping community. The last two chapters have described ways to study the Psalms. The purpose of the exercise is to find ways that will help the student to read the Psalms with understanding and to envision how a particular psalm can function in the life of the faith community.

Chapter 2 furnished organizational helps for studying psalms and described both the worship context out of which the

Psalms came and the literary context in which we read psalms. Chapter 3 has treated the Psalms' use of language. We have seen that, in a sense, these two chapters have rather different starting points. This chapter has simply begun with the text as it stands; chapter 2 related more to the cultural or socio-historical context from which the Psalms came. The student might be tempted simply to work on the rhetoric of the texts and ignore the matters of type/structure, setting, and shaping—matters that are sometimes more difficult. But psalm texts reflect the critical nature of such issues. Unfortunately, many studies that concentrate on poetic style in psalms have not been informed by the more historical studies and vice-versa. A study of the language of the Psalms, however, needs to pay attention to matters of origin in order to establish a context or perspective for interpretation. The interpreter otherwise runs the risk of missing the historical moorings to which the text bears witness. Historical analyses also need to be complemented with attention to the language of the text in its canonical form. Rhetorical analysis enables the student to move beyond questions of origin. In other words, the perspectives of chapters 2 and 3 need to inform each other and dialogue with each other. The reader needs to ask all four of the questions relevant for psalm interpretation. Each question is significant and accords a different kind of information indispensable for getting the full picture of a psalm. When the student has put these questions to a psalm, she or he can examine all the resultant information and begin to formulate a coherent view of the psalm. This integrative task may not be easy, but it is the final step in formulating the message of a text; and the task is impossible without the perspective of each of the questions used to study a psalm.

Our study, then, has offered beginning points for psalm interpretation. We have noted four questions to ask when examining a psalm:

1. What is the type/structure of the psalm?
2. How was the psalm used in worship?
3. How did the community "shape" the psalm?
4. To what end does the psalm use language—parallelism, divine names, repetition, "loaded" terms, figures of speech?

We need to keep these questions in mind when studying the Psalms. Then readers can combine consideration of these matters with close attention to the content of the various kinds of psalms. The next chapters will treat the major types of psalms with both content and our four questions in mind. These treatments of texts will apply our methods of psalm study and seek to present interpretive clues for students of the Psalms. First we will look at the laments.

Laments: Out of the Depths
— **4** ———————————————————

W e have been examining ways to interpret the Psalms. Now we come to the application of these methods. We begin with the lament psalms. A lament arises from the midst of distress and pleads with God for help. The Psalter as the "Book of Praises" offers praise to God in times of both divine presence and absence. The laments reflect that experience of God's absence. We begin with the laments because they reflect fundamental dimensions of human experience: suffering, despair, pain, hopelessness, and anguish. The Psalter reflects this harsher aspect of life when it includes more individual laments than any other psalm type. This chapter will explore the laments in relation to the four questions noted in chapters 2 and 3 as essential for psalm interpretation. The discussion will also consider more specifically the content of the laments and particular issues that arise in studying these psalms. The chapter will conclude with some sample treatments of laments and some comments on the significance of this psalm type.

Type and Structure

The chart below takes into account but one division among the laments—the distinction between *individual* and *community* psalms. Such a separation reflects the fact that the texts themselves distinguish between the individual worshiper and the congregation. Scholars have suggested various ways of grouping the lament psalms, and we will return to these proposals. For the moment, however, let us consider all the laments.

PSALMS OF LAMENT				
Individual Psalms				
3	22	40	62	102
4	25	42–43	63	109
5	26	51	64	120
6	27	52	69	130
7	28	54	70	140
9–10	31	55	71	141
11	35	56	77	142
13	36	57	86	143
16	38	59	88	
17	39	61	94	
Community Psalms				
12	58	80	106	137
14	60	83	108	
44	74	85	123	
53	79	90	126	

The lament psalms have a typical structure. Psalm 13 provides a good example.

I. **Invocation.** The introduction addresses the prayer to God (v. 1).

> How long, O LORD? Wilt thou forget me for ever?
> How long wilt thou hide thy face from me?

II. **Complaint.** This section describes, in a variety of ways, the crisis which has prompted the lament (v. 2).

> How long must I bear pain in my soul,
>   and have sorrow in my heart all the day?
> How long shall my enemy be exalted over me?

III. **Petition.** The worshiper then pleads for help (v. 3). A number of lament psalms include motivation(s) or reason(s) concerning why God should help (v. 4).

> Consider and answer me, O LORD my God;
>   lighten my eyes, lest I sleep the sleep of death;
> lest my enemy say, "I have prevailed over him";
>   lest my foes rejoice because I am shaken.

IV. **Conclusion.** The conclusion is usually positive. It may include an expression of confidence that God hears the prayer. This may include an expression of trust in God (v. 5) or a promise, a vow to offer praise to the God who delivers (v. 6). Sometimes the psalm concludes with that praise.

> But I have trusted in thy steadfast love;
>> my heart shall rejoice in thy salvation.
> I will sing to the LORD,
>> because he has dealt bountifully with me.

This structure does not appear in every lament psalm, but many of these psalms include these sections and in this order. Thus awareness of this typical structure can help in reading the laments.

Setting

We have already noted that some type of crisis occasions a lament. The superscription to Psalm 102 well describes the background for individual laments: "A prayer of one afflicted, when he is faint and pours out his complaint before the LORD." This superscription reflects the two parts of the setting from which the laments come—the crisis and the cultic setting of prayer.

The psalms describe the crisis as a sojourn in Sheol. Sheol is the world of the dead, the underworld, the dark, shadowy realm of death. The inhabitants of Sheol, who might be said to exist rather than to live, are even called "shades." The lament psalms describe the speaker as gripped by the power of Sheol or death, as trapped in a walled, fortified city with no hope of escape. Psalm 88 presents a compelling description of Sheol. The speaker is in the darkness and isolation of the Pit, a synonym for Sheol. Helplessness and terror characterize the experience of one gripped by the power of death.

The sojourn in Sheol is an effective, though highly figurative, way to describe the crisis behind the laments. There have been a variety of attempts to identify the crisis more specifically. Gunkel understood the primary crisis to be sickness. Other possibilities include the suggestion that the speaker suffers from the effects of false accusation or malicious gossip, or from oppression at the hand of unjust authorities. Another possibility is that the individual speaking represents the nation in the midst of a crisis affecting the whole community. A variety of possibilities present themselves, and it is not necessary to choose any one option for all the individual laments. The psalms do not speak of only one type of crisis; they describe material, mental, physical, and spiritual suffering. These various realities are often related and combined. In addition, the general language of the psalms often makes it difficult to be specific about the nature of the crisis. Some have preferred to apply the rather general term "persecution." While the general language of the laments causes difficulty in identifying the specific crisis behind the laments, it has the advantage of making the texts relevant to different people in a variety of crises. We will return to this perspective below.

The other part of the setting of the laments reflects the fact that these texts are prayers spoken in worship. Recent studies have suggested that the individual laments came from family or small group rituals.[1] Such a setting is entirely possible and would provide a bridge between the public and private recitation of psalms; however, various laments refer to worship activity as well as the community's history with God. The public use of these laments seems undeniably clear. The texts are, in any case, prayers used in rituals seeking deliverance from an imminent crisis. We will describe some of these rituals in the next section, but first we need to look at the community laments.

These psalms arose out of crises facing the whole nation. Military defeat surfaces several times. Psalm 137 reflects this type of setting in a specific way, the fall of Jerusalem in 587 BC. This defeat was traumatic for ancient Israel, and the psalm cries out for vindication. Crop disaster and societal corruption appear as the trouble in other community psalms. As with the individual laments, these texts also evolved from worship settings in which the community cried for God's help. The temple ritual of grief

---

[1]See Miller, *Interpreting*, 6, 7, for a convenient summary.

and trouble on public fasting days (1 Kgs 8:33–37) would require prayers resembling these psalms. Specific rituals commemorated the fall of Jerusalem, and community laments would have been included. Community laments were also part of regular worship days (e.g., the Day of Atonement) in which the ritual sought God's help. Lament psalms, both individual and community, arose from various rituals seeking God's help in the midst of a crisis facing the worshiper(s).

Studying the Laments

Our study has so far made only one formal distinction between the laments, the distinction between community and individual laments; but the interpreter can further organize the study of the laments into various sub-types. Such a procedure is particularly helpful with the individual laments, since any attempt to read all the individual laments in one sitting could become debilitating. A look at the various groupings of laments will open a way to consider the content of these psalms. One way of grouping the laments is according to setting.

(1) A number of laments appear to be *prayers offered by sick persons*. These prayers came from a ritual to seek help from God and may have included a family setting. Psalm 6 is likely a prayer from one who is sick:

> Be gracious to me, O LORD, for I am
>   languishing;
>   O LORD, heal me, for my bones are
>   troubled. . . .
> Turn, O LORD, save my life;
>   deliver me for the sake of thy steadfast
>   love. . . .
> My eye wastes away because of grief,
>   it grows weak because of all my foes.
>   (vv. 2, 4, 7)

(2) Other individual laments are *prayers of those falsely accused*. Evidence from the Old Testament supports the view that the temple was the location of some trials and that persons came

there to plead for some divine sign of acquittal. These psalms were prayed as a part of that proceeding. Psalm 7 is such a plea. Verses 3–5, an oath of self-imprecation, reflect such a setting.

> O LORD my God, if I have done this,
> if there is wrong in my hands,
> if I have requited my friend with evil
> or plundered my enemy without cause,
> let the enemy pursue me and overtake me,
> and let him trample my life to the ground,
> and lay my soul in the dust.

Also note the legal language in vv. 8 and 11.

> Yahweh judges the peoples;
> judge me, Yahweh, according to my
> righteousness
> and according to the integrity within me. . . .
> God is a righteous judge
> and a God who passes sentence every day.
> (my translation)

(3) Psalm 31 also appears to be a prayer in the face of false accusation, but in a different way. The problem is more general than legal and may reflect a setting involving malicious gossip against the worshiper. The psalm was used in a ritual seeking God's help in the face of such accusation.

> Let the lying lips be silent,
> which speak arrogantly against the righteous
> in pride and contempt. (v. 18, my
> translation)

Thus, some laments are *prayers of those facing malicious gossip*.

(4) Another way to categorize these last two types is as *psalms of innocence*. Psalms 7 and 31 fit this category, as do a number of laments. Psalm 17 claims innocence from an accusation. Psalm 26 also relates to a ritual of innocence. The worshiper claims innocence from a particular accusation and claims that she or he has been faithful to God.

> Vindicate me, O LORD, for I have walked in
> my integrity,

> and I have trusted in the L ORD without
>   wavering. . . .
> I wash my hands in innocence,
>   and go about thy altar, O L ORD. . . .
>   (Ps 26:1, 6)

(5) Other laments appear to be *pleas for asylum* in the temple. The sanctuary was a place of protection from evil pursuers. The worshiper in a psalm like Psalm 61 sought God's protection there until the crisis passed. So the text is a plea for asylum and a divine judgment in favor of the lamenter. Note the references in v. 3 to God's refuge and protection and to the safety of the tent (temple) in v. 4.

(6) Another group of laments might be called *prayers of the oppressed*. Psalm 94, for example, reflects a setting in which the speaker is among those facing injustice at the hand of civil authorities. The prayer calls for help in the midst of a crisis.

> They slay the widow and the sojourner,
>   and murder the fatherless. . .
> for justice will return to the righteous,
>   and all the upright in heart will follow it. . . .
> Can wicked rulers be allied with thee,
>   who frame mischief by statute?
> They band together against the life of the
>   righteous,
>   and condemn the innocent to death. (vv. 6,
>   15, 20–21)

(7) Still other laments are cultic prayers originating in a crisis situation; these prayers seek God's help, but they are difficult to put into a specific category. We might best describe them as *prayers from persecution*. Psalm 55 furnishes a good example of this kind of lament. The description of the crisis is quite general.

(8) We have already noted the psalms of innocence. This categorization begins with the worshiper's approach to God rather than the crisis behind the lament. The psalms of innocence are rather numerous in the Psalter. Less numerous, but still significant, are the *psalms of penitence*. These texts seek divine forgive-

ness and restoration to a relationship with God. Psalm 51 is well known for its desire for forgiveness, and Psalm 130 is often classified as a psalm of penitence. In this latter text, the speaker has sinned and seeks restoration and cleansing.

(9) Many of the individual laments are very difficult to categorize in a more specific way. The stereotypical language makes further categorization problematic. These psalms can simply be called *general laments.* Look at Psalm 22 as an example. The speaker appears to be sick, scorned, near death; the person has been falsely accused and oppressed in many ways. Poverty may even be in the picture, and the crowning blow is the perceived absence of God. The language of the text reflects a complex crisis, typical of the crises behind such laments. The worshiper brings the lament to God in the sanctuary and receives a favorable reply. The speaker then offers thanksgiving and sacrifice to God. Those present share a meal, and the worshiper offers exuberant praise to God. Psalm 22, then, is a kind of stereotypical lament. The language of the psalm makes any further categorization difficult; the crisis is not described in any specific way. This "open-endedness" of the text makes it adaptable for life.

We have listed several sub-types of individual laments. The question of organization is not quite so pressing with the seventeen community laments, but these texts also reflect a variety of settings. A military crisis is in the background of Psalm 60. This kind of crisis surfaces frequently in the community laments, especially in relation to the fall of Jerusalem. In addition, a crisis of famine is apparently behind Psalm 126. The people were in need of the blessing of harvest and cried to God for help. Corruption in society, with evil surrounding the faithful, provided the setting from which Psalm 12 arose. These comments reflect only a sampling of the various community laments.

The question of how one organizes a study of the lament psalms is difficult to answer. We have seen a variety of criteria that can be enlisted in the process, but no single way of grouping these psalms seems satisfactory. Walter Brueggemann has approached the classification of the Psalms in a different way.[2] He has sought to solve the dilemma by relating psalms more to functions in the community of faith than to literary types or particular settings. He uses the categories of *orientation, disorientation,* and new orientation. The laments are psalms of disorientation. Such a categorization certainly helps apply the psalms to the contemporary life of faith, but even Brueggemann's treatment offers little help with the further categorization of the laments. The issue is not settled, but this section has described a variety of ways in which the laments might be grouped. The discussion should at least help familiarize the student with the content of these psalms. The psalms in our list of laments share similarities in form and setting. This fact, along with the difficulty of further categorization, supports treating these texts as one psalm type.

The Enemies in the Laments

Other issues related to the laments need our attention; one question relates to the enemies mentioned in these texts. The Psalms describe the action and identity of those who seek to harm the righteous in a variety of ways. The descriptions are rather general, but students of the Psalms have suggested several identities for the enemies. Chapter 2 commented on the tendency of scholars in the last two centuries to identify the conflicting entities as opposing parties in early Judaism. Mowinckel suggested that the enemies were sorcerers, practitioners of black magic who had placed a curse upon the righteous person. This curse had brought about illness, and the worshiper prayed for restoration. Some psalms speak of the enemies as false accusers or as persecutors. The enemies in the community laments are usually national enemies, and some scholars have understood the enemies in the individual laments in the same way. Gunkel thought the laments were reacting against disease and distress. As mentioned above, Gunkel suggested that illness was the primary crisis behind the

---

[2]See Brueggemann, *Message of the Psalms.*

laments. Ancient Israel regarded illness as judgment because of sin; thus crises produced much tension, which produced strain in relationships. Gunkel then proposed that the righteous who prayed the psalms saw those who opposed them as wicked enemies. The result was the description in the Psalms of two stereotypical groups, righteous and wicked, or worshipers and enemies.

Gunkel's last observation carries the ring of truth. The enemies are described in rather general ways and thus are difficult to identify with any specificity. In addition, the identity of the enemies varies from psalm to psalm. The enemies in the community laments are different from those in the individual laments. The enemies in one individual lament may be characterized as false accusers and in another as those mocking one who is sick and thus perceived to be under judgment. There is no single answer to the question of the identity of the enemies in the laments. G. W. Anderson speaks of the "conventional monotony" and "confusing variety" in the description of the enemies.[3] These terms well characterize the issue. Consider Psalm 22:12, 16–21 as an example:

> Many bulls encompass me,
>   strong bulls of Bashan surround me. . . .
> Yea, dogs are round about me;
>   a company of evildoers encircle me;
>   they have pierced my hands and feet—
> I can count all my bones—
>   they stare and gloat over me;
> they divide my garments among them,
>   and for my raiment they cast lots.
> But thou, O Lord, be not far off!
>   O thou my help, hasten to my aid!
> Deliver my soul from the sword,
>   my life from the power of the dog!
> Save me from the mouth of the lion,
>   my afflicted soul from the horns of the wild oxen!

---

[3]See G. W. Anderson, "Enemies and Evildoers in the Book of Psalms," *BJRL* 48 (1965–66): 18ff.

With those kinds of images to describe the enemies, one can see why it becomes difficult to describe them with any precision. At the same time, this kind of stereotypical language makes the laments adaptable to many situations. Obviously the identity of the enemies in the laments can be problematic.

Another concern for many readers of the Psalms is that a number of these psalms contain prayers seeking vengeance on the enemies. Psalm 137 illustrates this feature for the community laments:

> Remember, O LORD, against the Edomites
>   the day of Jerusalem,
> how they said, "Rase it, rase it!
>   Down to its foundations!"
> O daughter of Babylon, you devastator!
>   Happy shall he be who requites you
>   with what you have done to us!
> Happy shall he be who takes your little ones
>   and dashes them against the rock! (vv. 7–9)

Psalm 109 exhibits the same feature in an individual lament. This prayer is unrelenting in its desire to have the enemy "cut off from the earth." These prayers seek God's judgment against the enemies.

Many readers simply ignore these psalms as distasteful and contrary to the ideals of their faith community. This course of action, however, would mean missing a significant part of the Hebrew Bible. These texts seek justice for a worshiper who has been wronged. The opening section of Psalm 109 describes this circumstance. The speakers of the Psalms exhibit a strong sense of justice and an awareness of what it means to be God's people. These passages, then, are part of the fight against injustice and the enemies of God and God's worshiper(s). In addition, these psalms are prayers addressed to God, not curses as they are sometimes called, and thus they leave any decision in the matter to God. The prayers seek God's help rather than invoking an impersonal, ritualized curse formula. In these prayers against the enemies, the worshiper does not destroy the enemy, but in a liberating act of faith, places the matter with God, the judge par excellence. God will decide, and the psalm pleads for God to decide against the enemies. The faith exhibited in these prayers includes a remarkable honesty. We will return to this matter below. The enemies in the laments present several difficult issues, and our discussion has only introduced the issues. Another question relates to the way the laments conclude.

The Conclusion of the Laments

Our analysis of the structure of laments indicated that most of them come to a positive conclusion. This positive word is so pervasive in the laments that it must be an established part of the psalm type. The transition from the trials of crisis to this positive word provides one of the most interesting topics in the study of the laments. Again, a number of possibilities present themselves.[4] It may be that these conclusions were added later or that the entire text was used later as a kind of thanksgiving for God's deliverance from the crisis. In most cases, however, the crisis seems still to be present, though there is a kind of pause before the transition—in anticipation of a word from God. Artur Weiser has suggested that the history of God's deliverance in ancient Israel has been brought to bear in these texts. The worshipers remembered God as the one who delivers and came to believe that God would also deliver them from the current crisis. A perspective like this is certainly possible for some laments, but it does not explain the transition to a positive conclusion in all the laments.

Another suggestion is that the simple use of the name "Yahweh" ensured the success of the ritual. A related possibility is called the psychological explanation: a kind of auto-suggestion, combined with the therapeutic venting of anger—which is certainly included in these texts—enables the speaker to move beyond the crisis. These suggestions minimize the involvement of

---

[4]See W. H. Bellinger, Jr., *Psalmody and Prophecy* (JSOTS 27; Sheffield: JSOT Press, 1984), 78–82; A. Weiser, *The Psalms. A Commentary* (Philadelphia: Westminster, 1962).

God in the process, a prospect foreign to these psalms. Others, however, point out that sudden shifts of mood are characteristic of prayer.

The most popular explanation of the sudden shift of mood from crisis to joy is that a word from God, an oracle, has been received by the worshiper. Joachim Begrich supported this view that a priestly oracle of salvation brought a word proclaiming hope for the future. This word signaled God's approaching, comforting presence and salvation. The word promised deliverance; the conclusion of the laments, then, is response to this oracle. Begrich found examples of such salvation oracles in Isaiah 41:8–16 and 44:2–5, oracles which the prophet borrowed from the worship of ancient Israel. Other Old Testament scholars have supported this view. Some caution is in order because the psalms do not as a matter of course contain oracles, but other Old Testament texts and parallel ancient Near Eastern materials attest to oracles like these. They were probably a part of ancient Israel's worship; this view offers the best available explanation of the sudden change of mood in the laments. The priest may have indeed proclaimed an oracle, even though the oracle inserted a "prophetic" element in the ritual since it called for a move away from hopelessness to hope in the coming deliverance of God. Gunkel suggested that the oracles originally provided the conclusion to the lament form. He further contended that the positive conclusion was developed in the lament form after the oracles were no longer in use as a means of indicating the positive conclusion of the ritual. The Old Testament's picture of ancient Israel's worship, however, would lend itself to the view that both oracle and grateful response to such a divine word were part of the ritual. The positive conclusions to the laments are a significant part of this psalm type. We will return to their theological significance.

Shaping in the Laments

Chapter 2 indicated that the community of faith shaped the Psalter in accordance with the life of faith. This process of shaping influenced the final form of both individual psalms and the entire book of Psalms. The concerns we noted in chapter 2 as operative generally for the Psalms are also at work in the laments.

(1) The previous section spoke of the pervasiveness in the laments of a positive conclusion, a conclusion that consistently speaks of *hope for the future.* The speakers of the laments stand between promise and fulfillment like the readers of these psalms. The laments are almost unanimously moving toward resolution of the crisis at hand. Psalm 6:8–10 well illustrate this part of the shape of the laments:

> Depart from me, all you workers of evil;
> for the LORD has heard the sound of my weeping.
> The LORD has heard my supplication;
> the LORD accepts my prayer.
> All my enemies shall be ashamed and sorely troubled;
> they shall turn back, and be put to shame in a
> moment.

(2) The same kind of movement is noticeable in *the organization of the Psalter.* The dominant psalm type in the first part of the Psalter is lament, and especially individual lament. The Psalter moves toward praise and the involvement of the entire community. The organization of the book reflects the movement in the life of faith from death to life, and the community has shaped its pilgrimage songs in line with that reality.

(3) A particular illustration of this movement from sorrow to joy is ancient Israel's experience in exile. Some community laments originated in relation to this crisis. Other laments have a more general referent, but have been shaped in such a way as to apply the psalm to the crisis of exile. Psalms 51 and 130 may reflect *influence from the exile.*

> Do good to Zion in thy good pleasure;
> rebuild the walls of Jerusalem,
> then wilt thou delight in right sacrifices,
> in burnt offerings and whole burnt offerings;
> then bulls will be offered on thy altar. (Ps 51:18–19)

> O Israel, hope in the LORD!
> For with the LORD there is steadfast love,
> and with him is plenteous redemption.

> And he will redeem Israel
>   from all his iniquities. (Ps 130:7-8)

(4) Psalm 130 also reflects how a number of individual laments are shaped so that they may be applied to the community. Psalm 25 is an individual psalm that seeks God's pardon from guilt. The last verse of the psalm adapts the prayer for congregational use.

> Redeem Israel, O God,
>   out of all his troubles.

Verses 6 and 7 of Psalm 61 also reflect this *community emphasis*. The prayer seeks protection; the references to the king as leader of the community apply the refuge theme to all of ancient Israel.

(5) The shaping of the Psalms so that they apply to settings beyond the original crisis is also evident in the *superscriptions*. Several of these relate laments to crises in the life of David.

> To the choirmaster: according to The Dove on Far-off Terebinths. A Miktam of David, when the Philistines seized him in Gath. (Ps 56)

> To the choirmaster: according to Do Not Destroy. A Miktam of David, when he fled from Saul, in the cave. (Ps 57)

In these superscriptions, David represents the person who is struggling with a crisis. This example of how the prayer fits during a time of trial helps readers of the psalm see how the lament applies to comparable times in their lives. Patrick Miller has used a similar helpful device in reading the laments by relating them to crises in the lives of other Old Testament figures, especially Jeremiah.[5] The laments are again adaptable for life.

(6) The most pervasive feature tying the laments to the life of faith is *the language of the Psalter*. We have already noted how general the language is; we have also seen that the laments related to rituals in ancient Israel. When the community no longer practiced these rituals, the people continued to use the

---

[5]See Miller, *Interpreting*, 48-63.

psalms. The language of the texts made it possible for many in various crises to apply the psalms to their own setting in life. Psalm 6 could be prayed by anyone who is sick or by anyone who is emotionally distraught. The same is true of Psalm 102. This openness or adaptability of psalm language is one of the major reasons the psalms have continued to influence persons of faith.

The laments thus give evidence of shaping by the community of faith, shaping that related to the needs of the worshiping community. The psalms were applied to various settings in life and were broadened to facilitate their usefulness for the continuing community of faith. In this way, the community tied the laments to the readers' pilgrimage of faith.

Rhetoric in the Laments

Chapter 3 emphasized the importance of the persuasive function of language in the Psalms. The role of language is especially noticeable in the laments. These psalms emerged from a crisis situation and fervently sought God's deliverance from that crisis. One of the significant rhetorical devices used in the laments is motivation. The lamenter often gives reasons why God should deliver.

> Consider and answer me, O LORD my God;
>   lighten my eyes, *lest I sleep the sleep of death;*
> *lest my enemy say, ''I have prevailed over him'';*
>   *lest my foes rejoice because I am shaken.* (Ps 13:3, 4)

> Help us, O God of our salvation,
>   *for the glory of thy name;*
> deliver us, and forgive our sins,
>   *for thy name's sake!* (Ps 79:9)

The motivation may be the trust of the speaker, penitence, the honor of God, or the crisis itself. All expressions look toward the purpose of the psalm—to persuade God to deliver. The "plot" of the text, then, is the movement through the trouble at hand to its resolution. The language in the laments is used exclusively in that context.

Since the laments are prayers addressed to God, the presence of divine names is noteworthy. Divine names often occur in strategic places and in ways that emphasize the relationship between worshiper and God. Note the examples from Psalms 13 and 79 above. Terms that traditionally describe ancient Israel's faith (unchanging love, faithfulness, righteousness, justice, covenant) occur frequently in these texts. They may describe the worshiper or God, the one who may deliver. The laments also often employ repetition in referring to the crisis or its cause, a recollection of God's past faithfulness to the people, or the mention of the need at hand—all seeking to persuade God to act on behalf of the speaker. To that same end, the laments also employ a variety of images—often to describe vividly the crisis as the worshipers' being closed in, to describe God's deliverance in terms of the freedom of being in an open and broad place, or to describe the enemies as wicked. These rhetorical devices are treated in the examples in the next section. The more general point, however, is that the laments use language vividly in order to persuade God to deliver. They also use echo effects as a means to draw the reader into the world of the text, a world structured around relationship with God.

Representative Laments

This chapter has said something about the laments as a group. The approach to these texts may be clearer if we illustrate with some particular psalms.

Psalm 6

1. *Type/Structure.* Psalm 6 is an individual lament that follows the typical lament structure. The text begins with address to Yahweh and then impressively alternates between petition and complaint.

> Yahweh, do not punish me in your anger
>   or chasten me in your wrath.
> Be gracious to me, Yahweh, for I am languishing;
>   heal me, Yahweh, for my bones are troubled.

And I am greatly dismayed
  but you, Yahweh—how long?
Turn, Yahweh, deliver me;
  save me for the sake of your unchanging love.
For there is no remembrance of you in death;
  in Sheol who will give praise to you?
I am weary with my sighing;
  every night I drench my bed with tears;
  I flood my couch with my weeping.
My eye wastes away from grief;
  it grows weak because of all my foes. (vv. 1-7, my
    translation)

The lamenter asks for God to deliver. One of the interesting aspects of this psalm is that the enemies do not surface until v. 7; they are, however, still in view in the psalm's conclusion.

Depart from me, all (you) evildoers,
  for Yahweh has heard the sound of my weeping.
Yahweh has heard my supplication;
  Yahweh has accepted my prayer.
All my enemies will be ashamed and greatly dismayed;
  they will turn back; they will be shamed in a
    moment. (vv. 8-10, my translation)

The conclusion is clearly set off from the remainder of the psalm and indicates that God has heard the worshiper's prayer and has responded favorably. The verses also speak of the decisive overthrow of the enemies, who have taken on major significance by the end of the psalm. The identity of the enemies is not clear, but their importance and their demise are. The verbs in the lament's conclusion indicate that God has heard the lament and will certainly bring salvation. This option seems more likely than one that argues that the conclusion was added after the deliverance had come to pass. Perhaps the worshiper received a salvation oracle after v. 7. At any rate, the psalm concludes on a positive note.

  2. Use in Worship. Now that we have seen the text of the psalm, we are in a better position to ask how the psalm was used in ancient Israel's worship. The psalm is a lament spoken in the midst of a crisis of major proportions. Verses 3, 6–8 contain some indications that the crisis may have been sickness. The language of the text makes it difficult to be very specific, but the likelihood is that Psalm 6 is a prayer that originated in a ritual seeking healing.[6] The ritual sought restoration and purification, since sickness was related to judgment from God. So this lament is a prayer of a person who is sick.

3. *Shaping.* The worshiping community has shaped the language of this lament in such a way, however, that the prayer is not limited to that original setting. Any worshiper facing a life-threatening crisis could make use of this prayer, even as the prophet Jeremiah drew from the language of illness to describe his problems with the prophetic task. Many persons in communities of faith through the centuries have faced tremendous crises and stood between promise and fulfillment as they prayed Psalm 6.

4. *Rhetoric.* The rhetoric of Psalm 6 is also effective. The speaker brings a crisis to God; the psalm is the plea. Its vivid description of trouble shores up the argument that God should act on behalf of the lamenter. God's honor and the potential demise of the speaker are also listed as reasons why God should answer. The conclusion of the psalm suggests that the crisis has been resolved. The divine name Yahweh appears several times in the plea for help and occurs three times in vv. 8, 9 to indicate a positive response. Note the correlation between the plea and the response. The "weeping" of v. 6 is heard in v. 8; the worshiper is dismayed in v. 3, the enemies in v. 10. The enemies seem to grow in importance as the psalm moves toward its *denouement.* Another significant term occurs in v. 4, חֶסֶד (*ḥesed*). This term signified for ancient Israel God's love, which does not change with circumstances. In Psalm 6 the plea is that God will act to bear witness that the divine graciousness is still operative. Another term worth noting is the word for "heard" in vv. 8, 9, שָׁמַע (*šāma'*). Yahweh has heard and granted the plea; this term often functions in the laments to indicate this. Finally, notice the psalm's picturesque

---

[6]See Mowinckel, *Psalms in Israel's Worship,* 2:1ff.

language, which describes the crisis, especially the weeping at night in v. 6. Equally powerful but quite incisive language portrays the resolution of the crisis in vv. 8–10. The language, and its parallel structures, also beckon readers to experience the weight of the crisis and its resolution.

Psalm 6 fervently pleads for Yahweh to delay no longer, but to act on behalf of this languishing worshiper. The alternative is death for the lamenter. God hears the prayer, a scene repeated many times throughout the history of faith communities.

Psalm 26

1. Type/Structure. To begin with, ask the question of type and structure. Psalm 26 is an individual lament. It begins with an address to Yahweh in the context of an introductory plea in vv. 1–3. The plea carries its own motivation; vv. 4 and 5 extend the motivation for God to answer the plea. Verses 6–8 provide yet additional motivation. Verses 9 and 10 present a plea for vindication, and the last section of the psalm, vv. 11 and 12, brings the text to a positive conclusion. The crisis that occasioned the psalm is implicit, but the text distinctly reflects some sort of trouble.

2. Use in worship. Such difficulty would be reflected in the psalm's role in worship. Verses 6–8, 12 reflect cultic use, and hints exist that the psalm may be a prayer of one who has been falsely accused. The person came to the temple to plead a case and to seek some sign of vindication, of acquittal, from God, the final judge. The psalm begins with a plea for vindication; the worshiper fears being counted among the wicked. Verse 2 hints of an oath of self-imprecation. We can understand much of the text as protestation of innocence, perhaps from some sort of accusation. The psalm does not explicitly describe the crisis, and so our identification of the type of ritual from which the psalm came must be tentative, but the psalm obviously relates to some type of cultic setting.

3. Shaping. While the psalm's connection with the cult seems clear, this lament is somewhat different from others. We might observe such differences while discussing the shaping of the text. Psalm 26 coheres well as a unit, as our analysis of its structure indicated; any editorial additions to the poem are unlikely. The place of the psalm within the Psalter, however, raises several issues. First, hear a translation of the text.

> Of David
> Vindicate me, Yahweh, for I have walked in my
>   integrity,
>   and in Yahweh I have trusted without wavering.
> Examine me, Yahweh, and try me;
>   test my inward parts and my heart.
> For your unchanging love is before my eyes,
>   and I walk in your faithfulness.
> I do not sit with false people,
>   and with dissemblers I do not associate.
> I hate the company of evildoers,
>   and with the wicked I do not sit.
> I wash my hands in innocence
>   and go about your altar, Yahweh,
> to sing aloud a confession of thanks
>   and to narrate all your wonderful acts.
> Yahweh, I love the habitation of your house
>   and the place for the dwelling of your glory.
> Do not take me away with sinners
>   or my life with the blood-guilty
> in whose hands is evil device
>   and whose right hand is full of bribe.
> But I walk in integrity;
>   free me and be gracious to me.
> My foot stands on level ground;
>   in assemblies I will bless Yahweh. (Psalm 26, my
>   translation)

(1) Verses 4 and 5 are reminiscent of Psalm 1, the introduction to the Psalter which characterizes the book as part of God's instruction or "torah" in the honest dialogue of faith. This connection indicates that Psalm 26 should also be understood as torah. (2) Psalm 26 also commends a life of integrity, and the worshiper contrasts himself or herself with the sinners described in vv. 9 and 10. The ethical concern is balanced in the psalm with an emphasis on the sanctuary, the place where the worshiping commu-

nity gathers to renew its trust in God and its integrity as a people. (3) Psalm 26 is a lament like many other psalms in the first part of the Psalter. Its positive conclusion indicates that the psalm speaker and reader are on the way towards resolving the crisis at hand. The text holds out hope for the future. (4) This text also exhibits typical psalm language. While it originated in a temple ritual, the language is also adaptable for life and a variety of circumstances. The language is intentionally general in order to facilitate its reinterpretation by the community of faith through the generations and its application to various life settings. Any worshiping community could appropriate this prayer as part of the dialogue of faith.

4. *Rhetoric.* Finally, what about the rhetoric of Psalm 26? The psalm is an especially artful composition. It uses various kinds of parallelism. Verses 4 and 5 exhibit a chiastic (AB B′A′) structure. The text consistently uses "Yahweh" as the divine name; the text begins and ends with the name. Verses 6–8 also emphasize the divine name since they focus on the place of the divine presence, the sanctuary. Other examples of repetition pepper the text. Frequent instances of the first person pronouns ("I," "me") are balanced with "your," indicating the relational aspect of the prayer. The text also underscores the innocence of the worshiper, especially in contrast to the evil enemies. Also notice the imperative verbs in the psalm: vindicate, examine, try, test, do not take away, free, be gracious—all commands that convey urgency in the plea. The repetition in the text also includes a number of the traditional terms of ancient Israel's faith. They especially indicate the worshiper's integrity and trust in Yahweh's חֶסֶד וֶאֱמֶת (*ḥesed we' ĕmet*), unchanging love and faithfulness. The worshiper encounters this reality in the sanctuary, the place of the glory of Yahweh, which is not only the temple but also a symbol of God's refuge. After being tested, the lamenter, at the conclusion of the lament, is brought to a broad and level place, away from the constriction of the current crisis. The central section of the psalm, vv. 6–8, emphasizes the sanctuary as a place of refuge, a place integral to the resolution of the crisis. At the end of Psalm 26, Yahweh views the speaker favorably.

Psalm 26, then, came from a ritual in which a person sought vindication in the midst of a crisis. The hope for vindication is in relationship with God, a relationship nurtured in worship and lived in *integrity*. Persons facing similar crises could appropriate this psalm for the life of faith.

Psalm 64

1. *Type/Structure.* Psalm 64 is an individual lament that begins with an introductory petition to Yahweh.

> Hear my voice, O God, when I complain;
>   preserve my life from fear of the enemy.
> Hide me from the secret plots of the wicked,
>   from the scheming crowd of evildoers. (vv. 2, 3, my
>   translation)

The psalm continues, in what might be called the complaint, with an extended description of these evildoers.

> who sharpen their tongues like swords,
>   who prepare bitter words as arrows
> to shoot at the innocent from ambush,
>   shooting at him suddenly and without fear.
> They hold fast to their evil word;
>   they talk of laying snares thinking, "Who can see
>   us?"
>   They devise injustices,
> "We have completed a shrewdly conceived plot."
>   For inward mind and heart are deep.
>   (vv. 4–7, my translation)

The conclusion of the psalm abruptly changes tone; the worshiper is suddenly delivered from the arrogant enemies he or she fears.

> But God will shoot them with (his) arrow;
>   suddenly their defeat will come
> and their tongues will cause it to fall upon them.
>   All who see them will wag their heads.
> Then all men will fear
>   and will declare God's act
>   and will ponder what he has done.

> Let the righteous rejoice in Yahweh
>   and seek refuge in him;
> let all the upright in heart glory. (vv. 8–11, my
>   translation)

The enemies are suddenly and publicly humiliated; their evil returns upon them. God has appointed judgment.

2. *Use in worship.* Most commentators relate Psalm 64 to some type of accusation by enemies. Verses 4 and 9 indicate that the enemies' weapons are words, and v. 5 signifies that the speaker is innocent. What the lamenter seeks is a sign confirming innocence. The enemies are liars, and the prayer looks for vindication. Yet, there is a lack of legal language; consequently, the accusation here might be characterized as malicious gossip. The prayer would then have come from a temple ritual seeking God's help in the face of such evil words.

3. *Shaping.* Psalm 64 follows a series of laments, but its positive conclusion leads to several psalms of a more hymnic nature. Perhaps the most striking thing about the shape of this psalm is the relationship between the crisis and the positive conclusion of the lament. The speaker clearly stands in the midst of a crisis looking to the future with hope. Also note that the language of the psalm is quite general. Its language makes it difficult to identify specifically the enemies and crisis, but it also enables other persons in similar crises to pray the psalm as part of their honest dialogue of faith.

4. *Rhetoric.* Since Psalm 64 is a part of the Elohistic Psalter (see pp. 10–11 in chapter 1), the name used for God is Elohim, except, interestingly, in the last verse, which exuberantly calls on the righteous to celebrate Yahweh's act of deliverance. The image of the hunter infuses the text. Initially the wicked hunt their innocent prey with bow and arrow, thinking they are unseen; and then God hunts the wicked and publicly humiliates them. The loaded terms in the psalm contribute to this theme with the sharp contrast between the righteous (the worshiper) and the wicked. Parallel lines accentuate the contrast. Especially noticeable is the correspondence between the complaint and the positive conclu-

sion of the text. God shoots his arrows, as did the wicked. Their tongues cause their defeat, their tongues in which they had placed so much confidence. Their evil rebounds on their heads. The enemies who thought they were unseen are publicly humiliated for all to see. This event brings hope for the faithful. The fortunes of lamenter and enemies are reversed. God has acted and the upright rejoice. The psalm's conflict between the worshiper and his or her enemies has become a conflict between God and those enemies, and the enemies are defeated. Psalm 64 bears witness to God as strong refuge in the face of destructive words, strong refuge encountered in the worshiping community.

Psalm 12

1. Type/Structure. Our illustrations of laments should also include a community lament. Even though individual laments outnumber community laments, the public nature of all these texts is evident by their use in worship; and the community also faced crises that affected all the people. Psalm 12 illustrates a community psalm. As part of an introductory plea, the psalm begins by addressing Yahweh. These verses also mirror the crisis from which the lament arose.

> Help, Yahweh, for the godly have vanished;
>> for the faithful have disappeared from among the
>>> sons of men.
> Everyone utters lies to his neighbor;
>> they speak with flattering lips and a double heart.
> May Yahweh cut off all flattering lips,
>> the tongue making great boasts,
> those who say, "With our tongue we will prevail;
>> our lips are with us; who is our master?"
>> (vv. 2-5, my translation)

Verses 6 and 7 reflect a distinct and sudden change of mood. In v. 6 Yahweh speaks in oracular form; the Lord will help the oppressed and faithful. Yahweh will arise and deliver them from the wicked. Verse 7 also expresses confidence in the divine word:

"Because of the oppression of the poor, because of the
    moaning of the needy,
   now I will arise," says Yahweh;
   "I will place (him) in the safety for which he pants."
The words of Yahweh are pure words,
    silver refined in a furnace on the ground,
    purified seven times. (vv. 6, 7, my translation)

The final verses indicate that protection for God's people is anticipated.

You, Yahweh, do protect them.
    Preserve us from this generation forever.
The wicked prowl around on every side,
    as evil is exalted among the sons of men.
      (vv. 8, 9, my translation)

2. Use in worship. The speaker faces a completely corrupt society; perhaps the ruling class is oppressing the poor. Decadence is the order of the day. Psalm 12 is a cultic cry in the midst of societal corruption, from the communal viewpoint. Mowinckel relates the psalm to the New Year festival.[7] Note that hope dramatically comes in a prophetic word in v. 6. The original setting of the psalm is an entirely corrupt society, and the psalm is a cultic cry for God's help.

3. Shaping. This psalm appears among several laments and is shaped in such a way that it is adaptable to crises, including societal corruption, throughout the life of the worshiping community. The language is quite general. While several commentators have suggested that the text originated under alien rule, this conclusion is not necessary. The prayer could relate to any crisis, including societal corruption. The text even blurs the distinction between individual and community. Psalm 12 also illustrates the standing of both speaker and reader in terms of hope for the future in the midst of crisis.

4. Rhetoric. Finally, we should note the rhetoric of the psalm. Verses 1–5 and 7–8 feature synonymous parallelism. The

---

[7]Ibid., 2:216.

divine name "Yahweh" is used most often in relation to a plea, but also to identify Yahweh's oracular word. Occurring with great frequency in the text is reference to words and lips and tongues and their power. Descriptions of enemies in the laments are common, and the enemies' words produce corruption in society. What is interesting is the use of "words" in v. 7 to describe Yahweh's words, which are pure and which will bring about safety for which the needy "moan." The image of the power of language dominates in the psalm, but notice v. 7: Yahweh's word has been purified, and thus can be trusted, and will bring about deliverance. The usual stock language to describe the wicked is employed in the psalm. Another loaded term is the word יֵשַׁע (yēše'), "safety, salvation," in v. 6. In this oracular word, Yahweh promises to place the worshiper in the sphere of salvation that Yahweh will produce.

Psalm 12 is a lament that seeks God's help in the midst of a corrupt society. In an oracular word, God promises that help in the face of evil. The text ends in a hopeful circumstance.

Conclusion

Our treatment of the laments concludes with some comments on the theological implications of these psalms. The lament psalms arise out of the depths of human experience, out of the difficulties of life. The prayers address a "thou" in the midst of crisis and thus operate in the context of an "I—thou" relationship with God.

> But thou, O LORD—how long? (Ps 6:3)

The question put to Yahweh is "how long?" because sometimes God is hidden, and yet with a strong community emphasis, ancient Israel continued addressing God even when God seemed absent or inactive. The dialogue persisted. God had initiated a relationship with ancient Israel, and in these texts the people call upon God to keep that relationship of faith intact. God risked in initiating that relationship so that the community might have life. These psalms plead for that reality to continue, and it does. These texts provide important material for believing communities; the laments demonstrate a bold and robust faith and bolster the life of faith, but often the worshiping community has missed this resource of faith because of fear. The texts are difficult and haunting; their honesty is brutal. And yet they provide much stimulation for the development of a deep faith. The community of faith needs to hear this word.

This description of the laments reflects one of the reasons a number of Psalms scholars now prefer the term "complaint" to that of "lament." These texts are not lament in the sense of resignation to the difficulty at hand. We have retained the most common terminology for the categorization, but remember that the text is in fact most often a complaint against God. It is a petition for God to do something, usually to maintain the divine part of the relationship with the worshiper(s). God initiated a relationship, and the community in worship seeks to hold God to the agreement. It complains so that God will act. This perspective is not true of all the laments. We noticed some psalms of penitence, those which seek forgiveness; the fault in those instances lay with ancient Israel. But most of the laments see the responsibility as now belonging to God; psalms of innocence dominate. The lamenters complain mightily against God and in so doing seek help.[8] Another way to describe this theological implication is that in the laments the worshipers are theologizing their current experience. They partake of the tradition which says that God delivers the believing community; in the current situation that deliverance is not at hand. Why? How long? These are the questions which the lamenters press upon the Lord to whom they relate. Why is the deliverance not at hand? Will it come? Must the worshiper(s) wait? Must the theological tradition change? In that context the community utters the laments.

The laments' amazing candor is sometimes shocking to the reader, but it is crucial to the honest dialogue of faith. The psalms do not bear witness to prayer "as it ought to be" but to

---

[8]See Brueggemann, *Praying the Psalms;* Westermann, *Praise and Lament;* Miller, *Interpreting,* 4–11.

brutally honest prayer from the depths of life. The laments demand that God relate to all of life, even to crises. The spirituality seen in the honest dialogue of faith in the laments is not weak or weary but bold and tough, even in the face of trial. An honest faith acknowledges life's realities. In the Psalms, no part of life is ever beyond dialogue with God.

The honest spirituality in the laments, therefore, is willing to encompass the pain which is inevitably part of the life of faith. Modern Westerners often find themselves seeking to avoid or deny pain, but the laments accept that pain is a significant and intrinsic part of life and seek to put that reality in the context of faith in God. And notice that the admission of pain is done in a public manner, even in the individual laments, for they were used as a part of public worship. The psalms recognize even before modern psychology that we do not deal with pain by ignoring it but by acknowledging it and moving through it. Faith, in these psalms, becomes a powerful resource in that battle. The psalms that seek vengeance fit here. They call God to the divine task of justice and take the desire for vengeance to the Lord who can act upon it. The laments thus do not ignore the pain of life, but put it in the context of faith in Yahweh.

Of particular importance at this point is the conclusion to which most of the laments come. The certainty that God hears the prayer is a dominant note in the laments. The Psalms have been called praise in the presence and absence of God. The laments deal with the experience of abandonment, and yet it is clear that they move to praise when in the midst of crisis; the laments end with hope. This aspect is essential in understanding these psalms. The laments cry out of the depths for God's help; God responds.

The laments nurture a powerful theology and faith in the context of worship. Their faith is a robust, bold one. These texts speak to God in such a way that the reader expects God's immediate activity; perhaps this perspective provides a clue as to why these psalms sometimes frighten many contemporary pilgrims of faith. The psalms call upon God to act as God should and deliver and bring justice as promised, and the speakers expect it to happen. The laments unabashedly insist that the deathly side of life be included in the honest dialogue of faith in God. These pilgrimage songs of faith articulate and nurture faith at the very depth of human experience.

Our discussion of these psalms' content and the various issues involved in their interpretation should help the reader tackle the task of studying the lament psalms in an open and faithful context. The movement of the laments from death to life, however, indicates that our journey through the Psalms is not finished; for the other major psalm category is praise, the psalms which embrace the joyful side of human experience in the life of faith. Our next chapter continues the discussion by treating those psalms.

Psalms of Praise: Enthroned on the Praises of Israel

5

We have been exploring the lament psalms. We move now to the psalms of praise, psalms that celebrate the joy in human experience. If the "Book of Praises" offers praise to God in the midst of divine absence and presence, the psalms to be examined in this chapter reflect the joy of God's presence. We will consider these psalms in light of the four issues primary for psalm interpretation and consider more fully the content of the psalms of praise. The chapter will also include some sample treatments of psalms of praise and conclude with comments on the significance of the praise in these psalms.

The structure of this chapter will differ slightly from that of chapter 4 primarily because of the work of Claus Westermann.[1] Westermann began to work on the Psalms in a concentration camp in Nazi Germany. The Psalms comforted him greatly, and he has contributed much to our understanding of these texts. He regards Psalms as a book of different kinds of praises. Westermann suggests that there are two basic categories of psalms: *plea* and *praise.* The life of faith and prayer is then lived between the poles reflected in these two types of psalms. The pleas are the laments we have already encountered. The pole at the other end of the

---

[1]See Westermann, *Praise and Lament.*

continuum is praise, and Westermann identifies two types of praise psalms: descriptive and declarative. Declarative psalms of praise form the link between lament and praise. Declarative psalms testify to the congregation or narrate for it a specific act of deliverance God has accomplished for the worshiper in trouble. The psalm expresses the worshiper's תּוֹדָה (*tôdâ*), a word of confession or thanksgiving to God for the deliverance. We will call these texts psalms of thanksgiving because they offer praise and thanks to God based on the deliverance the psalm narrates. Declarative psalms of praise are also related to the other type of praise Westermann identified, descriptive praise, which describes God as praiseworthy in more general terms: God as creator, sovereign, nurturer. The descriptive psalms of praise are more often categorized as hymns of praise. We will examine the two types of praise psalms in order, first looking at the declarative psalms of praise or psalms of thanksgiving. A list of these psalms follows.

PSALMS OF THANKSGIVING	
Individual Psalms	
30	92
34	116
41	118
66	138
Community Psalms	
67	124
75	129
107	136

Psalms of Thanksgiving

As with the lament psalms, our list makes a distinction between individual and community psalms, but for the moment, let us consider all of these declarative psalms of praise or thanksgiving psalms. These texts have a distinctive structure. Psalm 30 provides a good example.

I. **The introduction** proclaims the intent to give thanks and praise (vv. 1–5).

> I will extol thee, O LORD, for thou hast drawn me up,
> and hast not let my foes rejoice over me.
> O LORD my God, I cried to thee for help,
> and thou hast healed me.
> O LORD, thou hast brought up my soul from Sheol,
> restored me to life from among those gone down to
> the Pit.
> Sing praises to the LORD, O you his saints,
> and give thanks to his holy name.
> For his anger is but for a moment,
> and his favor is for a lifetime.
> Weeping may tarry for the night,
> but joy comes with the morning.

II. **The narrative** tells the story of the crisis (vv. 6, 7), the plea for help (vv. 8–10), and the deliverance (v. 11) so that others can also experience the power of this testimony.

The Distress

> As for me, I said in my prosperity,
> "I shall never be moved."
> By thy favor, O LORD,
> thou hadst established me as a strong mountain;
> thou didst hide thy face,
> I was dismayed.

The Prayer

> To thee, O LORD, I cried;
> and to the LORD I made supplication:
> "What profit is there in my death,
> if I go down to the Pit?
> Will the dust praise thee?
> Will it tell of thy faithfulness?
> Hear, O LORD, and be gracious to me!
> O LORD, be thou my helper!"

The Deliverance

> Thou hast turned for me my mourning into dancing;
> thou hast loosed my sackcloth
> and girded me with gladness . . .

III. **The conclusion** is a renewed vow of praise or testimony (v. 12).

> that my soul may praise thee and not be silent.
> O LORD my God, I will give thanks to thee for ever.

Psalms 116 and 118 provide a good picture of the worship setting of these psalms of thanksgiving. The setting is one of testimony to the God who delivers.

> I thank thee that thou hast answered me
> and hast become my salvation. (118:21)

Sacrifice often accompanied this thanksgiving.

> What shall I render to the LORD
> for all his bounty to me?
> I will lift up the cup of salvation
> and call on the name of the LORD.
> I will pay my vows to the LORD
> in the presence of all his people. . . .
> I will offer to thee the sacrifice of thanksgiving
> and call on the name of the LORD.
> I will pay my vows to the LORD
> in the presence of all his people,
> in the courts of the house of the LORD,
> in your midst, O Jerusalem.
> Praise the LORD! (116:12–14, 17–19)

The conclusion of the lament psalm often includes a vow to praise the God who delivers. The psalms of thanksgiving fulfill that vow. Laments are prayers for deliverance in the midst of trouble; psalms of thanksgiving are prayers of praise after God has delivered the worshiper(s).

As in the lament psalms, the sojourn in Sheol, the Pit, becomes the primary means for describing the crisis at hand. The power of death has gripped the speaker in such a way that fullness of life has been diminished, but God has now delivered the person(s) to wholeness of life. Because of this deliverance, the speaker offers praise to God, all in the context of the worshiping community, so that others can see the impact of God's action.

All of these psalms give thanksgiving to God for deliverance from a crisis. The community psalms relate to crises involving the whole nation: military defeat (Pss 75; 124; 129) and famine

(Ps 67). Psalm 107 illustrates a variety of crises: imprisonment, sickness, wilderness wandering, storms at sea, oppression, and famine; and Psalm 136 recounts the wonderful history of God's deliverance. Individuals also offered praise and thanksgiving for deliverance from crises: sickness and accusation (Pss 30; 41) and persecution (Ps 66). Psalm 138 reflects the history of God's delivering individuals from crisis.

Our discussion of the declarative or narrative psalms of praise has, up to this point, concentrated on the first two concerns of psalm interpretation: type/structure and setting. In chapters 2 and 3, we noted additional concerns: shaping and rhetoric. The worshiping community has shaped psalms and the Psalter in accordance with the life of faith. In chapter 4, we saw some of the characteristics reflective of that shaping; the psalms of thanksgiving also exhibit some of those features.

(1) *The language of the Psalter* is the first noticeable characteristic. Psalms 116 and 118 give evidence that they were related to cultic ceremonies with sacrifice and festal processions, and yet the language of these texts made it possible for the community to continue to use the psalms when the ritual settings were no longer practiced. The language is adaptable for use beyond its original cultic setting.

(2) Another characteristic of the psalms of thanksgiving is the interplay between individual and community. While a number of these texts relate to an individual's experience, the psalms also exhibit a significant *community emphasis*. Psalms 30:4 and 118:2 address the community, and the thanksgiving psalms include a number of other texts which use the setting of the psalm to teach the community. Psalm 107:33–43 lacks the refrains found in the rest of the psalm; these concluding verses have a "wisdom" tone in that they encourage the community, based on the experience of rescue, to learn of God's חֶסֶד (*ḥesed*), or unchanging love. Psalms 34 and 92 relate deliverance to righteousness. Other thanksgiving psalms urge the community to learn from history's witness to God's deliverance. Psalm 136 gives thanks for the history of God's delivering the people from Egypt; Psalm 66 also applies

the history of God's delivering to a specific individual crisis. These texts call the worshiping community to see—based upon particular narratives of crisis, prayer, and deliverance—that God still delivers.

(3) *The organization of the Psalter* indicates a movement toward the involvement of the entire community. The psalms referred to in the previous paragraph reflect a similar concern, and a number of the community psalms of thanksgiving are in the latter part of the book of Psalms.

(4) The interplay between individual and community and the application of psalms to settings beyond their original service of thanksgiving are also reflected in the *superscriptions* of Psalms 30, 34, and 92. Psalms 30 and 92 refer to cultic settings: "A Song at the dedication of the Temple" and "A Song for the Sabbath," while Psalm 34 refers to a representative setting in the life of David.

(5) The narrative psalms of praise also reflect the *hope for the future* we have seen in much of the Psalter. These texts give thanks for deliverance accomplished but also on the basis of that experience seek to encourage a community which lives between promise and fulfillment.

> O give thanks to the LORD, for he is good;
>   for his steadfast love endures for ever!
>
> Whoever is wise, let him give heed to these
>   things;
>   let men consider the steadfast love of the
>   LORD. (Ps 107:1, 43)

Chapter 3 emphasized the rhetoric of the Psalms. When noting the rhetoric of the narrative psalms of praise, the reader becomes aware that these texts give exuberant thanks and praise to God and use vivid language to that end. They frequently use the name "Yahweh" in direct address, indicating that the psalms are part of the dialogue and relationship of faith; as the cry of crisis is part of the dialogue of faith, so is the joy of thanksgiving. Joy also provides the major images of the thanksgiving psalms. The worshipers joyfully recount God's acts of redemption.

> It is good to give thanks to the LORD,
>   to sing praises to thy name, O Most High;
> to declare thy steadfast love in the morning,
>   and thy faithfulness by night,
> to the music of the lute and the harp,
>   to the melody of the lyre.
> For thou, O LORD, hast made me glad by thy work;
>   at the works of thy hands I sing for joy. (Ps 92:1-4)

Psalm 118:27 also refers to festal processions of joy. The thanksgiving psalms often repeat or echo these images of joy at the reversal of fortunes. The experience of deliverance is described as the move from death to life. The texts often use traditional terms from ancient Israel's faith; it is God's steadfast love and faithfulness which the worshipers encounter.

> I bow down toward thy holy temple
>   and give thanks to thy name for thy steadfast love
>   and thy faithfulness. . . . (Ps 138:2)

The refrain "for his steadfast love endures for ever" permeates Psalm 136; the refrain of Psalm 107 is also relevant.

> Then they cried to the LORD in their trouble,
>   and he delivered them from their distress. . . .
> Let them thank the LORD for his steadfast love,
>   for his wonderful works to the sons of men! (vv. 6, 8)

Yahweh has moved the worshipers out of the isolation and oppression of death.

> The snares of death encompassed me;
>   the pangs of Sheol laid hold on me;
>   I suffered distress and anguish. (Ps 116:3)

Yahweh's steadfast love has brought renewed life, and the worshiping community of faith responds with joyous thanksgiving.

The rhetoric of the thanksgiving psalms is thus in a framework similar to that of the laments. The crisis at hand has brought about a conflict involving worshiper, God, and enemies. The declarative psalms of praise reflect a resolution of the conflict: the words of these psalms offer praise and thanksgiving to God for deliverance; the crisis is effectively past. The narration of this conflict resolution determines the movement of these psalms and provides the spring from which their rhetoric flows.

Our treatment of the thanksgiving psalms has touched upon the four major issues of psalm interpretation: *type/structure, cultic setting, shaping,* and *rhetoric.* We have seen that the declarative, or narrative, psalms of praise celebrate the life and joy which Yahweh gives, fullness of life in the present. They exuberantly describe a powerful God who delivers and give thanks to that God.

> O taste and see that the LORD is good!
> Happy is the man who takes refuge in him! (Ps 34:8)

Hymns of Praise

The declarative psalms of praise provide a link between plea and praise in the Psalter. Such psalms are also related to the other psalms of praise Westermann identified, the descriptive psalms of praise. These psalms describe God as praiseworthy; they are the psalms often called hymns of praise. A list of these texts follows.

PSALMS OF PRAISE				
General Hymns				
29	103	114	135	147
33	105	115	139	149
68	111	117	145	150
100	113	134	146	
Creation Psalms		**Enthronement Psalms**		
8	104	47	97	
19	148	93	98	
65		95	99	
		96		
Zion Psalms		**Entrance Liturgies**		
46	84	15		
48	87	24		
76	122			
Hymns with Prophetic Warnings		**Trust Psalms**		
50		23	125	
81		91	131	
82		121		

Kingship
Ma/Ma/

Type and Structure

Our list divides these psalms of praise into several groups. We will look at the significance of those groupings a bit later. First, however, we consider all of these hymns as a whole and begin with the question of structure. The hymns have a typical structure which the brief Psalm 117 illustrates quite well.

I. **Introduction.** The introduction is a call to praise. Central is the word "hallelujah," an imperative calling the community to praise Yahweh. The introduction in Psalm 117 is a universal call to praise (v. 1).

> Praise the LORD, all nations!
> Extol him, all peoples!

II. **Body.** The body of the hymn gives the reason(s) for praising God. These sections can be rather lengthy, and the hymns express these reasons in a variety of ways. Psalm 23 praises God as shepherd, Psalm 98 as king, Psalm 46 as "our refuge." These descriptions are epithets, or titles, which convey a reason to praise God. Relative (who) clauses provide another means of expressing the reasons to praise God; Psalm 146 describes God as the one

> who made heaven and earth,
> the sea, and all that is in them;
> who keeps faith for ever;
> who executes justice for the oppressed;
> who gives food to the hungry. (vv. 6, 7)

Hymns also use Hebrew participles (indicating continuous action) to articulate the reason for praising God. Psalm 145:14–16 reflects such usage.

> The LORD upholds all who are falling,
> and raises up all who are bowed down.
> The eyes of all look to thee,
> and thou givest them their food in due season.
> Thou openest thy hand,
> thou satisfiest the desire of every living thing.

Psalm 117 uses a final, common way to give the reason for praising God: a phrase with the particle כִּי (kî) which means "for" or "because." This psalm proclaims the call to praise because of God's constant loyalty and faithfulness to the people (v. 2).

For (כִּי—*kî*) great is his steadfast love toward us;
and the faithfulness of the LORD endures for ever.

III. **Conclusion.** The conclusion of the hymn is a renewed call to praise, often a repetition of the introduction. Psalm 117 concludes as it began, with "hallelujah," "Praise the LORD!"

Scholars have labeled this practice of giving reasons for the praise as the *predicative style;* the body of the hymn predicates the reason for praise. Yahweh is the subject of the hymns, and the body of the text provides the reason for praising this God. While this structure is not obvious in all hymns of praise, many do contain this general pattern; moreover, attention to this style of praise can help in reading the hymns.

Setting

From what sort of setting would such hymns of praise originate? We observed that hymns such as Psalms 95 and 100 refer to acts in worship. Psalm 81:3 refers to "our feast day," and Psalms 24 and 48 refer to the temple. The setting is most likely during ancient Israel's regular and festival worship. First, the hymns give us a glimpse into the atmosphere of regular temple worship. These texts celebrate Yahweh's greatness in history. Yahweh delivers and Yahweh is present with the community in Zion; this presence sustains and instructs the faithful. Leviticus 23 and 24 give some indication of what ancient Israel's worship involved. Second, the history of Old Testament festivals is difficult to piece together, but there was periodic celebration, such as in the Feasts of Passover and Weeks, of God's having granted an abundant harvest and self-revelation. The Feast of Tabernacles reminded the community of Israel's deliverance from Egypt. This feast was a part of a fall festal complex that probably also extolled Yahweh's rule over creation.

It is not possible to affix one worship setting for all the hymns of praise. They reflect numerous cultic settings. Our treatment will be more specific when we survey the groups of hymns in the next section. At this point, it is sufficient to say that the hymns emerge from a context of praise in ancient Israel's regu-

lar worship and festivals. These hymns celebrate Yahweh's glory
and the manifestation of Yahweh's presence and activity to the
worshiping community of faith. The hymns express enthusiasm
for God's greatness in history and in nature. This God is present
in Zion, and the worship encounter with God enables wholeness in life and gives instruction for living.

Studying the Hymns

A reader can study the hymns of praise in different ways.
Chapter 2 suggested that we read the hymns according to the
groupings given in the list on pages 22–23. Our survey of the
hymns of praise will begin with that suggestion and combine it
with our analysis of the structure of these descriptive psalms of
praise. The groups of hymns give different reasons for praising
God; these reasons will frame our discussion of these texts.

(1) In the first part of this chapter, we investigated the
declarative psalms of praise. They portray Yahweh as the God who
delivers, and thus in the narrative portions of those psalms give
one reason for praising God: *God delivers from particular crises.*

(2) The general hymns of praise also portray Yahweh as
the God who delivers. These psalms celebrate *the history of God's
saving the people.* Here the congregation of ancient Israel remembered,
that is, lived again, this tradition of their salvation history. The
worship that was the backdrop for these texts recounted in a dramatic way this record of God's saving acts. In such worship experiences, the people could encounter in a renewed way the God
who delivers and see the impact of past events upon the present.

The festal Psalm 105 illustrates this reason for giving
praise to God. The introduction (vv. 1–6) calls the community to
praise God by rehearsing God's past great works. As the people
commemorate and dramatize this salvation history, they bear witness to the distinctiveness of Yahweh as the God who delivers.

> O give thanks to the LORD, call on his name,
>   make known his deeds among the peoples!
> Sing to him, sing praises to him,
>   tell of all his wonderful works! . . .

> Remember the wonderful works that he has done,
>   his miracles, and the judgments he uttered,
> O offspring of Abraham his servant,
>   sons of Jacob, his chosen ones! (vv. 1, 2, 5, 6)

The address in v. 6, with its mention of the ancestors, acts as the transition to the body of the hymn and offers the reason for praising God. The body of the hymn narrates the history of God's faithfulness to ancient Israel. It begins with God's faithfulness to the ancestral promise in Genesis, a promise of land and offspring. Beginning in v. 16 the psalm moves to a poetic recounting of the Joseph story and the sojourn in Egypt, and v. 24 speaks of the divine fulfillment in Egypt of the promise that Abraham would be blessed with descendants. The people were once oppressed; the psalm then recounts the story of Moses and Aaron and the divine struggle to deliver the people by way of the plagues and exodus. Verse 39 reminds the reader of God's providence in the wilderness, and the concluding verses of the psalm refer to God's gift of land. The psalm closes with a renewed call to praise: Praise the LORD! Psalm 105, then, recounts the record of God's delivering the people in the past as the reason for praising God in the present; the psalm enabled the worshiping community to encounter this powerful tradition.

Several other psalms share this tradition: Psalms 68, 111, 113, 114, 115, and 135. The accounts of God's delivering were formative stories for ancient Israel. In the worship reflected in these psalms, the community reenacted those stories as a means of seeing their contemporary relevance. God has in history demonstrated חֶסֶד וֶאֱמֶת (*ḥesed we' ĕmet*), unchanging love and faithfulness.

Psalm 139 also speaks of this God who is involved in the life of the faith community. While the text may have originated from a trial setting (vv. 19–24), it begins by offering praise to the God who knows the worshiper (vv. 1–6), who is present (vv. 7–12), and who grants protection (vv. 13–18). This psalm as well as the historical hymns describe God as relating to the community in a dynamic way.

The first two reasons for praising God, then, have to do with the acts of God: deliverance from a crisis and the history of God's delivering ancient Israel. Both groups of texts, the thanksgiving psalms and the general hymns, describe God as the one who delivers. Psalm 139 helps provide transition to those hymns that portray God as the one who is present to bless. Other groups of hymns give additional reasons to praise such a God.

(3) The creation psalms supply a specific reason for praising God: *God creates.* Psalm 8 illustrates this emphasis. It begins with the praise of God and affirms that God has created strength even out of weakness. Next the psalmist marvels at creation, signified by the starry hosts of the night sky and wonder of the existence of humankind.

> When I look at thy heavens, the work of thy fingers,
>   the moon and the stars which thou hast established;
> what is man that thou art mindful of him,
>   and the son of man that thou dost care for him? (vv.
>   3, 4)

Yahweh has closed the vast gap between creator and the created and given dominion to women and men.

> Yet thou hast made him little less than God,
>   and dost crown him with glory and honor.
> Thou hast given him dominion over the works of thy
>   hands;
>   thou hast put all things under his feet. . . . (vv. 5, 6)

The psalm proceeds according to the order of creation in Genesis 1; suddenly it stops and returns to the introduction and praise of God. The psalm praises not the creation but the creator.
Psalm 19 is also a creation hymn.

> The heavens are telling the glory of God;
>   and the firmament proclaims his handiwork. (v. 1)

The emphasis on how the creation reveals God continues in vv. 2–6. Such revelation is then linked with God's תּוֹרָה (*tôrâ*), or instruction. God's instruction plays a vital role in some other psalms. Psalm 65 also speaks of God's universal blessing in the fruitfulness of nature, but it combines this emphasis with a description of God as the one who comes to deliver (v. 5). Psalms 8, 19, and

65 demonstrate that one of the central reasons for giving praise to God in the Psalms is that God is creator.

(4) The hymns picture God as creator, and as the creator who continues to rule over the creation. Such a portrayal of Yahweh is especially evident in the enthronement psalms. This group of psalms provides another reason for praising God: *God is king.* These psalms call upon the congregation to praise Yahweh with a new song because Yahweh rules over creation, over the earth, over the creatures upon the earth, and over the nations. Psalm 93 speaks of the majesty of this king and again connects creation with law. These hymns are great acts of rejoicing.

> Say among the nations, "The LORD reigns!
>   Yea, the world is established, it shall never be moved;
>   he will judge the peoples with equity."
> Let the heavens be glad, and let the earth rejoice;
>   let the sea roar, and all that fills it;
>   let the field exult, and everything in it!
> Then shall all the trees of the wood sing for joy
>   before the LORD, for he comes,
>   for he comes to judge the earth.
> He will judge the world with righteousness,
>   and the peoples with his truth. (Ps 96:10–13)

The poetic imagery honors God's kingly rule over creation as a reason to offer praise.

This theme, along with the emphasis on God as creator, was probably observed as part of the fall festal complex in ancient Israel. We recall that some sort of fall festival was a part of ancient Israel's sacred calendar; however, the history and nature of the festival have been debated by a number of scholars.[2] Some scholars see the emphasis on creation, some on covenant, some on the choice of Zion as the seat of God's presence and the Davidic monarchy. The enthronement psalms in the Psalter do seem

---

[2]For a helpful summary, see Clements, *One Hundred Years*, 85–87 and A. A. Anderson, *Psalms* (NCB; 2 vols.; London: Marshall, Morgan & Scott, 1972), 1:51ff.

to reflect a joyous cultic setting that enables the congregation to encounter again the kingship of God. The fall festival may well have included such an emphasis and may have been the original cultic setting for this group of psalms.

(5) The question of where God is king brings us to the next group of hymns, the *Zion psalms*, and to the next reason for praising God. God is king in Zion, Jerusalem, the location of the temple, the special place of the divine presence. As the home of festivals and as symbol of the presence of Yahweh, the temple was central for ancient Israel. The Zion psalms honor *God's presence with the people* as a reason for praise. The place of the divine presence was the site of life-renewing worship for the community. The Psalter contains songs for the pilgrimage to Zion, psalms that proclaim the beauty of that place and the desire to be there.

> I was glad when they said to me,
>   "Let us go to the house of the LORD!" (Ps 122:1)
>
> How lovely is thy dwelling place,
>   O LORD of hosts!
> My soul longs, yea, faints
>   for the courts of the LORD;
> my heart and flesh sing for joy
>   to the living God. (Ps 84:1, 2)

In the next chapter, we will examine the close associations between David and Zion. At this point, Yahweh's investment in Zion as the divine dwelling place is at the forefront. Psalms 46 and 48 speak of God's protection of Zion in the face of attack. Psalm 46 describes Zion as the place from which flows the river of life.

> There is a river whose streams make glad the city of
>   God,
>   the holy habitation of the Most High.
> God is in the midst of her, she shall not be moved;
>   God will help her right early. (vv. 4, 5)

God's life-giving presence is in Zion. Psalm 48 also speaks of Zion as the dwelling of Yahweh from which flows sustenance for life. Mount Sinai had been the mountain of God. Now Yahweh is present with the people and speaks from Mount Zion, the city of the great king (v. 2). This verse also locates Zion "in the far north" (צָפוֹן—*ṣāpôn*). The reference is to Mount Zaphon in the north, the dwelling place of the high God, the source of the waters of life. Mount Zion is now this life-giving divine dwelling and the place from which Yahweh speaks to ancient Israel. Psalm 48 reflects the community's dramatic portrayal, in the temple, of Yahweh's protection of the divine dwelling place.

> All we had heard we saw with our own eyes
>   in the city of the LORD of Hosts,
>   in the city of our God,
>   the city which God plants firm for evermore.
> O God, we re-enact the story of thy true love within
>   thy temple. . . . (vv. 8, 9, NEB)

God is present with the people, and they see this protecting presence in Zion (v. 12). The psalm offers festal praise to the God who guards against the powers of disorder and chaos. Yahweh has created and remains sovereign over the creation and all within it. The Zion psalms celebrate God's watchful presence; these psalms demonstrate the centrality of Zion for the life of ancient Israel.

Two other psalms deal with the question of who is qualified to worship on Zion; these are the entrance liturgies, Psalms 15 and 24. The texts reflect a setting in which pilgrims inquire concerning who may worship in the temple.

> Who shall ascend the hill of the LORD?
>   And who shall stand in his holy place? (Ps 24:3)

The priest answers with a word of instruction, a "torah," and puts the answer in terms of ethical living.

> He who has clean hands and a pure heart,
>   who does not lift up his soul to what is false,
>   and does not swear deceitfully. (Ps 24:4)

This emphasis on social ethics is a noteworthy prophetic word that underscores the Old Testament concern for a proper relationship between worship and life. The latter part of Psalm 24 also portrays Yahweh's entrance into worship. So these two entrance liturgies also speak of Yahweh as present with the people in Zion.

The first two reasons for praising Yahweh relate to God's activity to deliver; the three subsequent reasons relate to God's presence to bless: God creates, rules, and is present with the community. This God who blesses grants the power to grow and prosper in the world.

(6) The Entrance liturgies furnish a good point of transition to the next reason for giving praise to God. They include a prophetic word, which is instruction from Yahweh. Our list of the hymns of praise includes an additional group, *hymns with prophetic warnings*. These prophetic texts demonstrate another reason for offering praise to the God who is present with the people: *God provides instruction for the community*. For example, Psalm 50:4–15, urging loyalty to God, calls the people to faith, and vv. 16–23 chide the wicked for their disdain of God's instruction. Psalm 81, which is similar to Psalm 95, an enthronement psalm, well illustrates God's instruction for the people. The psalm begins with a hymnic call to praise that reflects a festival setting.

> Blow the trumpet at the new moon,
>   at the full moon, on our feast day.
> For it is a statute for Israel,
>   an ordinance of the God of Jacob. (Ps 81:3, 4)

The blowing of the trumpet could easily refer to New Year's and the fall festal complex, though the reference to Egypt in v. 5 could refer to either Tabernacles or Passover. The last line of v. 5—"I hear a voice I had not known"—indicates that prophetic instruction follows. The worship leader first reminds the community of God's past goodness toward them; God delivered them from oppression in Egypt and initiated relationship with them. Verses 11–16 then call for response on the part of the people, a response of loyalty, which has been lacking. The prophetic warning thus calls the people to repent and live in loyal relationship with God.

> O that my people would listen to me,
>   that Israel would walk in my ways! (v. 13)

The warning summons the community to follow God's instruction. The instruction is associated with the word given at Mount Sinai. God there initiated a relationship with ancient Israel, and now God calls the people to respond to that relationship in faithfulness. The call to obedience in Psalm 81 comes from Zion. The relationship between God's rule from Zion and God's law or instruction in Psalms 19 and 93 has been noted; the Prophets also echo these themes.

The Old Testament calls ancient Israel to live as a people in covenant relationship with Yahweh, and Old Testament texts that reflect a worship tradition also reflect that theological perspective. As in Joshua 24, the community was to renew regularly its covenant loyalty to God. The celebrations of Passover, the Feast of Weeks, and the Feast of Tabernacles in all likelihood included such an emphasis. The ritual of the Day of Atonement also implies renewal of relationship with Yahweh, and at some point the community came to observe this ceremony, as well as the New Year, along with the Feast of Tabernacles. The hymns with prophetic warning reflect such a background; in them praise and exhortation interact. God, this God who is creator and king in the midst of the community, has initiated relationship with ancient Israel and, in these hymns, instructs the community how to respond in that faith relationship. Such help for living adds further substance to the call for the people to give praise to God. These psalms, then, are also hymns of praise and have underlying them the complex of traditions or themes associated with God as creator and king, the one who blesses from Zion.

(7) The *trust psalms* also reflect the tradition of the God who is present in Zion to bless. They tender an additional reason to offer praise: *God is trustworthy.* God's record is proof. The famous Twenty-third Psalm with its emphasis on God as shepherd and host illustrates this theme. A psalm of trust seeks to nurture faith and trust as realities at the center of the community's life. Psalm 23 describes Yahweh as a shepherd in the midst of crisis.

> Even though I walk through the valley of the shadow
>   of death,
>   I fear no evil;

> for thou art with me;
> 　thy rod and thy staff,
> 　they comfort me. (v. 4)

The latter part of the text portrays God as the host who gives protection.

> Thou preparest a table before me
> 　in the presence of my enemies;
> thou anointest my head with oil,
> 　my cup overflows. (v. 5)

God has demonstrated חֶסֶד (*hesed*), unswerving love for the community of faith. We have noted this theme in other psalms of praise. The trust psalms rejoice over the community's experience of God's trustworthiness; the congregation has learned to hope in Yahweh, who has demonstrated loyalty to the people in a variety of circumstances. These psalms, in what is also a prophetic theme, call the people to continue to trust in God. God's demonstration of trustworthiness affords a final reason for praise. These psalms describe the God who can be trusted as the one who is present in Zion; they thus resonate with other hymns praising God as the one who is present to bless. We saw in chapter 2 that Gunkel categorized the trust psalms in connection with the lament psalms, and there is evidence to support such a connection. Our study, however, suggests placing the trust psalms among the hymns because of their hymnic quality; they praise and honor God's trustworthiness.

　　The hymns call the worshiping community to praise the God who comes to deliver and the God who is present to bless. These texts give a variety of reasons for praising the God who blesses: God has created, rules the creation, is present with the people in Zion, instructs the people in faith, and continues to demonstrate trustworthiness. Portrayals of God—as one who redeems from crises and who has a history of saving the people—extol Yahweh as the one who comes to deliver. Such hymns, both descriptive and declarative, rejoice in the full life given by Yahweh. This brief survey of the hymns, or descriptive psalms of praise, based on the reasons they offer for praising God, is related to the form and setting of the hymns. Now, we turn our attention to forces at work when the psalms of praise took their shape as a part of our Psalter.

Shaping in the Hymns

In chapter 2, we noted numerous concerns at work as the community shaped the Psalms in accordance with the life of faith. A number of those concerns were operative as the laments and thanksgiving psalms came to be part of the Psalter. The hymns reveal similar concerns.

(1) *The organization of the Psalter* suggests part of the significance of the hymns of praise for the life of faith. The first half of the Psalter concentrates on lament. Praise is the dominant theme of the second half of the Psalter. The life of faith moves toward the praise of God, toward joyful response to the full life God gives, and so does the "Book of Praises."

(2) We have also seen that the Psalter moves toward the involvement of the entire community; the first half of the Psalter emphasizes individual psalms, while the last half concentrates on community texts. A *community emphasis* pervades the hymns; few of them are psalms of individuals. Even "hallelujah," the imperative call to praise, is in the plural, which suggests a community context.

(3) Another way the community has applied the hymns to the life of faith is with *the language of the Psalter.* I have suggested that these texts originated in connection with various festivals and regular worship settings in ancient Israel. The texts, however, are not limited to those settings, as indicated by the fact that the community continued to treasure and use the psalms when they no longer practiced the rituals. The worshiping community still can use meaningfully the psalms celebrating Yahweh's kingship. Psalm 23 still nurtures trust in people centuries after its composition. One of the primary reasons the Psalms continue to be popular among people of faith is the adaptability of psalm language.

(4) The hymns also reflect a vibrant *hope for the future.* Psalm 46 boldly claims confidence in the face of opposition.

> God is our refuge and strength,
>> a very present help in trouble.
> Therefore we will not fear though the earth should
>> change,
>> though the mountains shake in the heart of the sea.
>> (vv. 1, 2)

The enthronement psalms look to the future with great hope in the rule of God.

> Let the sea roar, and all that fills it;
>> the world and those who dwell in it!
> Let the floods clap their hands;
>> let the hills sing for joy together
> before the LORD, for he comes
>> to judge the earth.
> He will judge the world with righteousness,
>> and the peoples with equity. (Ps 98:7-9)

The Psalter also concludes with a great flourish of hopeful praise. Psalm 150, an extended and rich call to praise, reflects the joy of life in relationship with God.

> Let everything that breathes praise the LORD!
> Praise the LORD! (v. 6)

Just as with the laments and declarative psalms of praise, the descriptive psalms of praise also give evidence of shaping by the community according to the needs of its life and worship. For centuries the hymns have been important for worshiping communities. Associating these texts finally with the pilgrimage of faith made such relevance possible for future readers.

Rhetoric in the Hymns

Our treatments of both the laments and the thanksgiving psalms alluded to their gripping use of language. The language is no less vivid in the hymns; the conceptual framework for studying the rhetoric of the hymns, however, is less obvious. On the one hand, laments and thanksgiving psalms offer a glimpse of conflict in the midst of crisis, and frequently of conflict resolution. The hymns, on the other hand, do not originate from settings of crisis; and yet on closer examination, the structure of hymns does arouse in the reader a question, if not a dilemma. The hymns summon the community to praise; will its members respond? That is the hope in which the hymns use persuasive language. They seek to encourage ancient Israel to give praise to Yahweh by enumerating reasons why the congregation should praise Yahweh, and then the hymns renew the call to praise. In the very act of giving the reasons for praising God, the worshiping community accomplishes the purpose of praise.

The hymns enlist rhetorical devices in the attempt to encourage praise. One is *repetition*. Psalm 150 is the climactic call for all to praise God. "Praise him" appears nine consecutive times at the beginning of lines of the psalm to urge the praise of God. Note the psalm's parallelism. Psalm 29 begins with three occurrences of "ascribe to the LORD" appropriate glory and then describes "the voice of the LORD" in seven ways to show that God has exercised great power for the community, a convincing reason to praise Yahweh. The hymns display a kind of echo effect that often brings to mind other hymns. The Zion psalms rely upon similar rhetoric, while most of the enthronement psalms are grouped together and begin similarly; and most use common themes, language, and imagery. The divine names, both Yahweh and God, are frequently repeated.

The hymns also *exploit traditional terms* of ancient Israel's faith. We have already seen that the general hymns often recount God's delivering the people from distress. The hymns also take advantage of traditional descriptions of God,

who made heaven and earth,
   the sea, and all that is in them;
who keeps faith for ever;
   who executes justice for the oppressed;
   who gives food to the hungry. (Ps 146:6, 7)

God is creator and savior. God's demonstration of trustworthiness is also part of the community's stock language about God, as is God's protecting presence on Zion. The hymns are replete with images of God as the one who delivers and as the one who undergirds and protects. We have seen imagery that inspires enthusiasm in expectation of the coming of God in the enthronement psalms. The Zion psalms relate God's powerful protection of Zion by recounting God's faithfulness to deliver in the face of the powers of chaos. And the trust psalms employ elegant images to nurture trust in Yahweh.

> But I have calmed and quieted my soul,
>> like a child quieted at its mother's breast;
>> like a child that is quieted is my soul (Ps 131:2).

Such rhetoric attempts to convince the community to praise God. The next section will study the rhetoric of certain psalms, but this section has provided enough illustrations to show the persuasive use of language in the hymns.

Representative Hymns

(1) *Psalm 100* is a good example of a general hymn of praise. Our first concern is type and structure. The text begins with the call to praise.

> Make a joyful noise to the LORD, all the lands!
>> Serve the LORD with gladness!
>> Come into his presence with singing! (vv. 1, 2)

The next verse calls the hearer to know Yahweh and then moves toward giving a reason for offering praise to God.

> Know that the LORD is God!
>> It is he that made us, and we are his;
>> we are his people, and the sheep of his pasture. (v. 3)

The last two verses illustrate well the predicative style of praise with its call to praise followed by the reason for praising God, expressed with a כִּי (*kî*) phrase.

> Enter his gates with thanksgiving,
>> and his courts with praise!
>> Give thanks to him, bless his name!
> For (כִּי—*kî*) the LORD is good;
>> his steadfast love endures for ever,
>> and his faithfulness to all generations. (vv. 4, 5)

The community owes its life to God and continues to encounter God's unchanging love and faithfulness as God supplies wholeness for the people. Note the impressive alternation between call to praise (vv. 1, 2, 4) and motivation for that praise (vv. 3, 5).

Following the question of type and structure comes the question of setting. In line with Mowinckel's description of the language of the Psalms, we can notice that Psalm 100 refers to cultic acts. Verse 2 speaks of coming into God's presence, into the temple, and v. 4 has a similar emphasis with mention of Yahweh's gates and courts. Thus the psalm has the air of a call to worship, probably connected with some sort of procession into the sanctuary. The references in vv. 3 and 5 to God's past acts on behalf of the community would fit the emphases of ancient Israel's festival calendar, perhaps especially the fall festivals. The fact that the psalm follows a collection of enthronement psalms lends support to this theory, but the careful reader would not want to go beyond this tentative suggestion of a specific cultic setting for the psalm because the psalm is so general in its praise of Yahweh. However, that the text had moorings in community worship is clear.

This comment leads to a discussion of the way the community has shaped Psalm 100 for the life of faith. The language of the text certainly transcends its original cultic setting; contemporary communities of faith still adapt the psalm to their worship settings. The superscription ties the text to worship, a central act in the community's life of faith. The text also has a community emphasis with its encompassing call to worship and its emphasis on God's creation of the people (v. 3). Finally, consider the place of the psalm in the Psalter. It follows a collection of enthronement psalms—celebrations of God's kingship—with a joyful word of praise to this king. Psalm 101, a royal psalm on the Davidic king in Jerusalem, comes next. The community rejoices in Yahweh as king and in Yahweh's just representative. Psalm 100 is then a strong word of praise concluding the enthronement psalms.

We observed earlier that the psalm focuses on a call to praise. It uses persuasive rhetoric to garner a response to that call and in turn to offer praise to God. The divine name is always

Yahweh, the special Hebrew name for God. Each verse contains
the name Yahweh, and v. 4 also refers to "his name." Yahweh
is the subject of the praise, and words of joy and thanksgiving
permeate the text. As we noted, the psalm is associated with the
place of worship (v. 4). Verse 3 refers to God's making the people,
and the final verse echoes a frequent emphasis in the Psalter:
Yahweh's חֶסֶד וֶאֱמֶת (*ḥesed we' ĕmet*), unchanging love and faithfulness. These terms reminded the audience of the history of
God's constant loyalty to the people. Finally, notice the image of
shepherd in v. 3, another reminder of God's benevolent care for
the people. In sum, Psalm 100 is an enthusiastic invitation to
praise Yahweh in worship; the sovereign of the universe also
serves as shepherd and guide for the community that listens and
obeys.

(2) *Psalm 46* supplies another good example of a descriptive psalm of praise, praising Yahweh as the one who protects
the temple city. This hymn of praise is a Zion psalm. It utilizes
a great many epithets to praise Yahweh as the one who is present
to protect the divine dwelling and ancient Israel. The text consists of three stanzas, with a refrain at the end of the second and
third stanzas. The first stanza indicates that the community of
Zion faces the power of chaos.

> God is our refuge and strength,
>   a very present help in trouble.
> Therefore we will not fear though the earth should
>   change,
>   though the mountains shake in the heart of the sea;
>   though its waters roar and foam,
>   though the mountains tremble with its tumult. (vv.
>   1–3)[3]

The description of the forces of disorder continues in the second
stanza.

---

[3] "*Selah*" appears after each stanza. The meaning of the word
is uncertain, but it may indicate the time for an instrumental interlude,
a time for instruments to "lift up their voices."

> There is a river whose streams make glad the city of
>   God,
>   the holy habitation of the Most High.
> God is in the midst of her, she shall not be moved;
>   God will help her right early.
> The nations rage, the kingdoms totter;
>   he utters his voice, the earth melts.
> The LORD of hosts is with us;
>   the God of Jacob is our refuge. (vv. 4-7)

God is present as refuge. The title "Lord of hosts," or Yahweh of armies, depicts Yahweh as a warrior who fights the powers of chaos. The hosts may be the heavenly hosts, messengers of God or heavenly bodies, or the hosts of ancient Israel's army. In any case, Yahweh protects Zion and for this blessing is praised. Yahweh is "a mighty fortress" who helps early; deliverance often came in the morning. The third stanza brings this emphasis to a conclusion.

> Come behold the works of the LORD,
>   how he has wrought desolations in the earth.
> He makes wars cease to the end of the earth;
>   he breaks the bow, and shatters the spear,
>   he burns the chariots with fire!
> "Be still, and know that I am God.
>   I am exalted among the nations,
>   I am exalted in the earth!"
> The LORD of hosts is with us;
>   the God of Jacob is our refuge. (vv. 8-11)

Yahweh defeats the enemies and destroys war. Verse 10 calls for recognition that God is the one who brings peace, and the psalm concludes in v. 11 with the refrain.

The question of setting for Psalm 46 raises a number of interesting issues. The background of the text is clearly a threat to Zion. The personal/historical approach to the Psalms looked for a historical event from which the psalm originated. The text makes it very difficult to specify any such event. Much more likely is the possibility that the attack is a representative or typical one enacted as a part of ancient Israel's worship. The text proclaims Yahweh as the one who is present to protect Zion from the powers of chaos and disorder, whether they be encountered as the earth changing and mountains shaking (v. 2) or as the nations raging (v. 6). God is the sovereign creator who rules in Zion. The significance of Zion also serves as strategic background for understanding the text. Zion was the capital of the united kingdom and became a key symbol for the Davidic kingdom and for ancient Israel. We will see its political significance in the next chapter, but it also became home for the temple and ark of the covenant and was thus a central symbol of God's presence among the people. It was pointed out earlier that Zion was acknowledged as a dwelling place for the high God who sustains life. That explains the reference to a river (v. 4), not a physical river—Jerusalem does not contain one—but the river of life that flows from the abode of Yahweh. The mention of Zion in Psalm 46 and the text's association with other hymns celebrating the God who is present to bless from Zion make it likely that the psalm comes from a special setting in ancient Israel's worship. Since Mowinckel, many have suggested the fall festivals as the setting; some setting honoring Yahweh as the creator who rules from Zion would be appropriate, but the text does not permit much insight beyond that.

The community has shaped the text by placing it with similar psalms. Psalm 44 is a community lament, and Psalm 45 a royal psalm. Psalm 47 is an enthronement psalm, and Psalm 48 another Zion psalm. The language of the text also ensures that the psalm transcends its initial setting. The language is quite adaptable for other settings affirming faith in God as "a mighty fortress." Communities of faith continue to intone its words. Once more the psalm proclaims a powerful hope for the future of the community.

Finally, a full reading of Psalm 46 should consider its use of language. We should recall the symbolic significance of Zion as the place of worship and the place of divine dwelling. This common theme helps hold the three stanzas together, as does reference to "the earth" in each. In stanza one, the earth shakes, moves, and totters, and the waters roar and foam; in stanza two, the nations rage and totter, and the earth melts. In both cases, God protects from chaos. The image of a safe refuge in the face of a devastating earthquake in the first stanza or in the face of raging enemy nations in the second makes the praise of God even more persuasive. The third stanza brings such an emphasis to a climax by depicting this ruling God as destroying war and its tools (v. 9). Note the echo effect in the last two lines of v. 10. The psalm concludes with a refrain (containing divine names) that emphasizes God's powerful and protecting presence for Zion.

(3) A final text to explore is *Psalm 23*. We will again discuss each of the four issues relevant to psalm interpretation. First is the issue of *type and structure*. Our list of the hymns has the Twenty-third Psalm under the hymns of praise as a trust psalm. In chapter 2, we pointed out that Gunkel suggested that the psalms of trust developed from the laments. The expression of trust in some texts has been expanded and has become the entire psalm. Psalm 23 certainly conveys trust and has some sort of crisis in its background. There are, consequently, reasons for associating the text with lament and thanksgiving psalms. However, the text suggests that the crisis is past and that the psalm's purpose is to offer praise to the God who has demonstrated trustworthiness in the past. In that sense it gives a reason to praise God by way of the epithet "shepherd" and calls upon others in the congregation to join in trusting such a God. The text displays a more hymnic quality about it; it joins in the adoration or praise of God, and the conclusion of the psalm associates it with Zion, a common referent in the hymns. Thus we study this psalm along with other hymns of praise, though it does depart from the typical hymnic form.

Second, we will examine its *setting*. A crisis is in the background, as the first four verses attest, though it is difficult to determine the exact nature of the problem.

> The LORD is my shepherd, I shall not want;
>> he makes me lie down in green pastures.
> He leads me beside still waters;
>> he restores my soul.
> He leads me in paths of righteousness
>> for his name's sake.

> Even though I walk through the valley of the shadow
>   of death,
>   I fear no evil;
>   for thou art with me;
>   thy rod and thy staff,
>   they comfort me. (vv. 1–4)

The last two verses suggest some type of cultic setting, perhaps a meal, which looks back on the trouble and praises God for being trustworthy in the face of the difficulty.

> Thou preparest a table before me
>   in the presence of my enemies;
> thou anointest my head with oil,
>   my cup overflows.
> Surely goodness and mercy shall follow me
>   all the days of my life;
> and I shall dwell in the house of the LORD
>   for ever. (vv. 5, 6)

This cultic setting supports our categorization of the text.

Third is the matter of *shaping*. The setting shifts from an individual crisis to a more general setting that urges others to join in trusting Yahweh. The language of the psalm also promotes this community emphasis as it transcends the original setting of the text. Faith communities throughout the generations have found this text to offer hope for life; the images of the psalm communicate to the pilgrimage of faith in multiple settings involving trust in God.

The *rhetoric* of Psalm 23 is its most dominant feature. The psalm is set off in the first and last verses with the divine name Yahweh; these verses highlight the import of the psalm since they introduce the major images in the text: God as shepherd and host. These images reflect the movement of the psalm. Shepherd is used first and put in the context of the risk of changing pastures and following new paths, but this shepherd gives guidance and comfort and leads his flock to life, even in the face of threats. The deepest darkness does not overcome the flock. Even life's darkest experiences bear witness to Yahweh's faithfulness. In the latter part of the psalm, Yahweh is the host who provides table and oil (symbolic of joy) in the face of threat and weariness, so much so that kindness, rather than enemies, becomes the reality that pursues the speaker. Yahweh serves as host in the temple with the worshiping community. The setting evokes an overflow of praise and trust. The psalm centers on the relationship with "thou" (Yahweh); pronouns refer to Yahweh, the giver of life and the basis of trust, even in the face of trouble. Such a picture of Yahweh is very much in line with the tradition of ancient Israel. Psalm 23, then, nurtures trust by creating a vivid portrait of faith in the context of the praise of God in worship.

Conclusion

Our treatment of the psalms of praise will conclude with some comments on the theological implications of these texts. The central instruction of the hymns is "hallelujah," praise Yahweh. The psalms call the community to praise God. In the last chapter, we encountered ancient Israel's pleas in the absence of God; the psalms of praise celebrate the life-giving presence of God. The psalms of praise are also interpreting life in light of the faith tradition, and in these texts the integration of faith and reality is complete. God grants fullness of life and so the community rejoices. The act of praise completes the experience of wholeness, and including the community in praise furthers its significance. In this role the psalms of praise comprise a major part of ancient Israel's pilgrimage songs of faith.

We have seen two kind of psalms of praise, declarative and descriptive. The declarative or narrative psalms of praise tell the story of how Yahweh has delivered from a crisis and offer appropriate thanksgiving. These psalms hark back to the pleas of the laments; in the thanksgiving psalms, Yahweh has heard the prayer and delivered the petitioner. Such declarative praise is connected with the psalms of praise that describe God. These texts speak of God as creator, king, trustworthy one, instructor, present one, and deliverer. All of these psalms of petition and praise comprise the community's pilgrimage songs of faith, and all are important to the life of faith. The psalms of praise then complete our view of ancient Israel's praise in the absence and presence of God.

These psalms of praise describe God in two primary ways: as the God who comes to deliver and as the God who is present to bless.[4] The psalms of thanksgiving narrate how God has delivered from crises, and the general hymns of praise recount the history of God's delivering the people. The other hymns describe God as the one who blesses: God has created life and continues to rule over it as king; this king is present in Zion with the people and instructs them in the life of faith; the God present in Zion has demonstrated trustworthiness. This God is not aloof, but is actively involved in the daily life of the community. This active involvement explains the dominant note of hope and joy in these psalms.

The praise of God in the Psalms also gives insight concerning the nature of praise. First, praise is always substantive. The psalms furnish a reason to praise God. These texts exhibit great depth and richness and connection to the fullness of human experience. Contemporary worshipers need the experience of hope and joy—and hope and joy of real substance. Second, the psalms of praise greatly enhance our understanding of how to offer praise to God. How do these psalms give praise to God? They recount what God has done and how God has been present. One praises God by narrating and describing God's involvement in the world. Thus the community praises God, deepens its faith, bears witness to God, and invites others to the life-giving act of praise. That kind of praise, as opposed to shallow antics, is most effective. Third, the praise of God in the Psalms is honest; the pain of the laments is candidly real, and the uninhibited worship in the psalms of praise arises out of genuine delight in God's goodness. Worshipers are not repressed by self-consciousness, because in worship, the community in the act of praise encoun-

---

[4]See C. Westermann, *What Does the Old Testament Say About God?* (Atlanta: John Knox, 1979).

ters the living God. The congregation responds to God and comes away renewed for the journey of faith.

The psalms of praise then also nurture a bold faith, one that does not hesitate to offer unrestrained praise to God. Many contemporaries find such an experience alien, and this is no doubt part of the reason they avoid serious study of the Psalter. The biblical version of the life of faith insists that God still delivers and blesses and thus that the worshiping community of faith joyfully sings praise to God. God is greatly to be praised. These psalms then proclaim and nurture faith at the core of the community's life. The Psalter ends,

> Let everything that breathes praise the LORD!
> Praise the LORD!

Our treatment of the psalms of praise and the various issues involved in their intrepretation should help the reader study these psalms and grow from them. But our journey through the Psalter is not yet complete. In the course of studying some of the hymns, we mentioned the royal psalms. These texts also had a vital relation to the life of the community. Our next chapter considers these psalms.

Royal Psalms: A Covenant with My Chosen One, David My Servant

— 6

Our study has, along with Claus Westermann, suggested that there are two basic types of psalms—praise and lament (in Westermann's parlance "plea"). Our classification of the Psalms, however, also lists two other types, royal psalms and wisdom psalms. These two categories, while including only a few psalms, do enhance our picture of the Psalter as a whole and are sufficiently different that they require separate treatment. This chapter and the next will consider them in order. The royal psalms come first; these psalms deserve separate consideration because they reflect influential settings and hopes in the life of ancient Israel. I have argued that four issues should shape our study of the Psalms: type/structure, setting, shaping, and rhetoric. This chapter will treat each of these concerns.

		ROYAL PSALMS	
2	21	89	132
18	45	101	144
20	72	110	

Type and Structure

The first question is whether it is appropriate to include royal psalms among the types of psalms. The psalms of lament and praise are literary types in the strict sense, but the royal psalms are not. Our list of these psalms includes a variety of literary forms. The common characteristic that holds the category together is the king; the psalms relate to different settings in the life of the Jerusalem king. Because the king held a distinctive and prominent position in the life of the worshiping community, and because this group of psalms makes its own contribution to our understanding of a variety of themes and concerns in the Psalter, it makes sense to treat these texts separately. So while "royal psalm" is not actually a literary type, there is justification for including it in our treatment of the various classes of psalms.

The next question we confront is, How many psalms should be included among the royal psalms? This question relates to a long-standing debate in psalm study: the identity of the "I" in the Psalter. In the last century, R. Smend suggested that the "I" represented the nation of Israel. His view challenged earlier scholars who related the Psalms to conflicts in the formative Judaism of the late Old Testament period. Smend's view was expanded by Harris Birkeland, who argued that the clearest identification of enemies in lament psalms was the national enemies referred to in the community laments. Since the description of the enemies in other psalms was similar, Birkeland concluded that the enemies in the Psalms were national enemies and that many of the laments were prayers spoken on behalf of the nation by a leader, perhaps the king. A number of psalms certainly share common characteristics, but there is also variety in the Psalter that Birkeland does not take into full account. In his view, the pattern by which psalms were composed overshadows the setting or composer from which a psalm came.

Mowinckel has followed the position of Birkeland to some degree. He notes the alternation of "I" and "we" and the military terminology used in a number of psalms, especially laments. He suggests that in these texts the king is functioning as the representative of ancient Israel and is speaking for Israel in the midst of a political and military crisis. Later these texts were democratized so they could be used by others. Accordingly Mowinckel argues that some laments are truly individual psalms; others are royal laments. This position is more cautious than Birkeland's; and while the king was certainly a prominent figure in the worshiping community, one wonders why texts quite similar in form and content should relate to rather different backgrounds, one royal and one individual. Recently John Eaton has argued for the royal interpretation of many psalms. His view is that earlier attempts to suggest settings for these psalms, especially laments, have failed; our treatment of the laments has suggested otherwise. Eaton presents a variety of arguments for his position that a royal setting provides the best background for understanding quite a number of the psalms. Several of his arguments relate to the importance of the monarchy in ancient Israel. Some psalm scholars thus take the view that the number of royal psalms is notably higher than eleven.[1]

Our list of royal psalms, following the work of Emil Balla, however, suggests a different view. In the debate with Smend, Balla argued convincingly that there are genuine individual psalms. Certainly the king was an important figure in pre-exilic Jerusalem, but the religion of the day did not exclude the place of individuals. In fact, the canonical Psalter took its final shape long after the demise of the Davidic monarchy. This fact argues against interpreting large numbers of psalms as royal compositions. Hope for the future seems to be the primary reason royal texts were included in the Psalter. A number of the psalms do alternate between first and third person in the midst of the text, but this practice appears to be common in the Old Testament. The weight of the evidence, then, suggests that a psalm should only be categorized as "royal" if the text itself makes that categorization necessary. Our list reflects that position.

Part of the problem inherent in this question is that the language of these texts is rather generic and the interpreter finds

---

[1]See Bellinger, *Psalmody and Prophecy*, 28–31.

it difficult to delineate a cultic setting. The reader of the Psalms senses the conventional monotony in the texts, but also encounters a confusing variety; the texts are not all alike, even in their descriptions of the enemies. A division between royal psalms and the other psalms treated in chapters 4 and 5 is thus tenable and followed in this chapter. Our treatment of these eleven psalms should provide an overall view of royal psalmody as well as the place of the king in ancient Israel. The two preceding chapters have concentrated on the place of individual and community; now our concern is the primary leader of the people.

As we saw above, the royal psalms include a variety of forms—lament and thanksgiving, along with prayers in relation to battle and even to a royal wedding. Several of these psalms also relate to the king's place in office and the basis of his rule. It is the common royal background, however, that unifies the group of psalms and to which our attention now turns.

Setting

The king is the common denominator for these eleven texts; therefore, recognizing the place of the king in ancient Israelite society is indispensable for interpreting these psalms. The king was a substantial figure in pre-exilic Jerusalem. He ruled as God's representative on earth and spoke to the people in that role. At the same time, the king, because of his special relation with God, represented the people in addressing God. The king had a kind of intermediary role. This view of kingship needs to be seen in the context of other monarchies in the ancient Near East. For example, the Egyptian pharaohs were considered divine. For ancient Israel, in contrast, the king was chosen by God, but the king remained human. The king ruled over the people in Jerusalem as God's representative, and God guaranteed the monarch's rule and kingdom. The Davidic kings, then, were the political rulers in Jerusalem; but they also held a central place in the religious life of the community. They were closely aligned with the temple and were leaders of worship. This view of kingship developed over a period of time in ancient Israel, but it seems to be the background of the royal psalms.

These psalms relate to public worship and the role of the king in worship. They reflect diverse settings in the public life of the king, both of the Davidic line of kings and of the particular king ruling at the time the psalm was used. Several of the psalms relate to the king's coronation and to the rights and responsibilities of his position. One royal composition celebrates the wedding of the king; others pray for the king in a time of threat.

Some of these psalms concern themes associated with Zion like those in the psalms of praise, and a number of scholars have used these texts to reconstruct a particular royal ritual in Jerusalem related to the autumn festival.[2] Aubrey Johnson has reconstructed a temple ritual in which the king, serving as representative of the people, died and then rose to celebrate victory over the powers of chaos, thereby renewing creation. Johnson used the royal psalms as well as parallel material from the ancient Near East to describe this ritual. Aage Bentzen also suggested that it was a ritual that dramatically depicted the king in battle (and ultimately in victory) for the people. The royal psalms that speak of the king's preparation for battle as well as those in which the royal figure faces the threat of defeat were, in Bentzen's view, part of this ritual. The monarch, again reflected in some of the royal compositions, was ultimately victorious and was escorted to the temple for enthronement. All such reconstructions are, of course, hypothetical, but they do offer a setting for the royal psalms and certainly reflect the centrality of the king during the time of the monarchy and his essential role in temple worship. The problems with discovering a particular historical setting for the royal psalms are insurmountable, and while we may not be able to describe a particular royal ritual out of which these psalms came, the texts do seem to re-

---

[2]See A. Johnson, *Sacral Kingship in Ancient Israel* (Cardiff: University of Wales Press, 1955); A. Bentzen, *King and Messiah* (Lutterworth Studies in Church and Bible; London: Lutterworth, 1955).

flect settings in the public life of the Davidic monarch. A number of these settings involved temple rituals.[3]

A Look at the Royal Psalms

Our discussion of the classification of the royal psalms and their background and cultic setting should put us in a position to briefly survey the eleven psalms in this category. Several of these texts relate to the beginning of the king's rule. Psalm 2 celebrates the coronation of the king. As is often the case with a change in leadership in an empire, vassals rebel against the new ruler. Psalm 2 depicts such a rebellion. Because this rebellion is against the Davidic king who has been chosen by Yahweh, however, the rebellion is also against the rule of God. God laughs at the futility of rebellion and declares once again the divine choice of the Davidic line to rule in Jerusalem-Zion. Beginning in v. 7 the king speaks and recounts God's decree to him concerning his reign. The king has, with coronation, become God's adopted son. God, therefore, guarantees the monarch's authority and rule; rebels will fall. The conclusion of the psalm urges the kings of the earth to submit to the Davidic king as the representative of Yahweh, the giver of life and death. Psalm 110 also indicates that Yahweh is with the king and guarantees victory over the king's enemies. God's choice of the monarchical line is firm, which puts the king in special relationship with God, thereby guaranteeing strength and victory. The last line of v. 4—"You are a priest for ever after the order of Melchizedek"—casts the king as a priestly figure, but the tenor of this text is very much one of the military victor, the one for whom God guarantees shattering, almost brutal victory.

Psalm 132 also extols God's choice of the king, though in a broader context. The psalm begins by recounting David's end-

---

[3]Because we have little explicit information on royal rituals in Jerusalem, the current tendency among scholars is to deemphasize such ritual reconstructions. There is also less enthusiasm for considering large numbers of psalms to be royal compositions.

less search for the ark of the covenant and his attempts to recover the ark for Jerusalem. David's forces found the ark, and it
eventually came to rest in Jerusalem and the temple; the psalm
celebrates the placing of the ark in Jerusalem-Zion as hope of
God's presence. Verses 8–10 petition Yahweh to be present there
for the people. The response to that petition is in vv. 11–12 and
is a commemoration of the Davidic covenant: God has made a
firm decision that David and his sons will rule as God's representatives over the people in Jerusalem, the abode of the ark, the
primary symbol of Yahweh's presence. The Davidic line is not the
only choice God has made, however, for God has also chosen
Zion as home. God will rest there and rule from there, guaranteeing the Davidic monarchy. From the place of the divine
presence on Zion, God will also provide fullness of life, blessing
for the congregation and its leaders. So Psalm 132 celebrates the
choice of Zion and David.

Psalms 72 and 101 take our consideration of the royal
psalms a step further. The first of these texts is in the form of
a prayer, a prayer for the king, which concentrates on the king's
responsibility to bring justice. As leader of the people, the monarch is to guarantee justice and righteousness.

> Give the king thy justice, O God
>   and thy righteousness to the royal son!
> May he judge thy people with righteousness,
>   and thy poor with justice!
> Let the mountains bear prosperity for the people,
>   and the hills, in righteousness!
> May he defend the cause of the poor of the people,
>   give deliverance to the needy,
>   and crush the oppressor! (vv. 1–4)

From such righteousness on the part of the king would come renewal, victory, and abundance for the monarch and the people.

> For he delivers the needy when he calls,
>   the poor and him who has no helper.
> He has pity on the weak and the needy,
>   and saves the lives of the needy.
> From oppression and violence he redeems their life;
>   and precious is their blood in his sight. (vv. 12–14)

A just and righteous monarch is the channel of blessing for the people, and the psalm prays that the king will achieve this royal ideal and live long. Psalm 101 is a companion text. It serves as a kind of oath of office that the king will execute justice. The ruler promises loyalty, justice, and integrity and takes an oath to lead the people in righteousness and truth. These royal psalms thus clearly set forth the ideal of a just king.

Another group of royal psalms concerns the king's part in battle. Psalm 20 prays for the king's victory in battle; the text proclaims that such victory will come from the God of Zion.

> May he send you help from the sanctuary,
>   and give you support from Zion! . . .
>
> May we shout for joy over your victory,
>   and in the name of our God set up our banners!
> May the LORD fulfil all your petitions! (vv. 2, 5)

The psalm concludes with a firm confidence that God will give the victory; perhaps a sign of this victory came between v. 5 and v. 6. The first part of Psalm 21 sounds as if God has already granted the victory to the king. These introductory verses, however, form the basis for the promise of victory in vv. 8–12.

> For you will put them to flight;
>   you will aim at their faces with your bows. (v. 12)

In Psalms 89 and 144, the king is in the midst of battle. The leader faces defeat in Psalm 89. The text begins with a long section that celebrates in hymnic form the covenant Yahweh made with David.

> Thou hast said, "I have made a covenant with my
>   chosen one,
> I have sworn to David my servant. . . ." (v. 3)

In the present, however, that promise is threatened by the prospect of military defeat (vv. 38–45). The psalm then petitions Yahweh to help the king in the face of this crisis; thus the text functions as a royal lament. Psalm 144 also seeks the power of Yahweh to give victory to the Davidic monarch (vv. 10, 11). Verses 12–15 imply that such royal victory could mean prosperity for the community, and thus the whole nation desires the victory. The righteous, victorious king is the channel of prosperity for the people. In Psalm 18, God has granted the deliverance that the king has sought, and the psalm offers thanksgiving in an exalted hymnic style. The psalm is best understood as a royal thanksgiving song, as the conclusion indicates.

> For this I will extol thee, O LORD, among the nations,
>   and sing praises to thy name.
> Great triumphs he gives to his king,
>   and shows steadfast love to his anointed,
>   to David and his descendants for ever. (vv. 49, 50)

A final royal text, Psalm 45, pertains to the king's wedding. The monarch is described in a majestic, complimentary way as the one whom God has chosen and blessed. The text also describes the bride as a beautiful and graceful woman, who is to provide blessing to the king and thus to the community. The psalm seeks blessing for the royal couple. This text also supports the view that the royal psalms speak of the royal ideal in ancient Israel, an ideal often unfulfilled.

Shaping

We have seen that the community shaped the psalms of lament and praise in accord with the life of faith. Shaping is no less clear in the royal psalms. Since we have now taken a look at these texts, what forces can we notice that were at work as these psalms came to their final form in the Psalter?

(1) When considering the *organization of the Psalter*, the first matter to notice is that the royal psalms are not preserved in a collection but are placed throughout ancient Israel's "Book of Praises." The placement of the texts does not seem to have special significance, though Psalm 2, as we have seen, is part of the introduction to the Psalter, and Psalms 72 and 89 do conclude the second and third books of the Psalter.

(2) The most striking aspect of the shaping of the royal psalms is their interpretation in the canonical form of the Psalter.

At the time of canonization (ca. 250 BC), there was no Davidic king in Jerusalem, and so these texts likely spoke of the community's *hope for the future.* God would yet bring one to fulfill the Davidic ideal embodied in these texts, and this king would make blessing possible for the faith community (Pss 72; 144). So a *community emphasis* is discernible in these as well as other psalms, and while the texts still clearly reflect a setting in relation to the Davidic king in Jerusalem, the language also makes possible a wider community referent. In this way, the royal psalms also partake of the adaptable *language of the Psalter.* With such shaping the worshiping community has continued for centuries to appropriate the royal psalms in a beneficial way.

(3) The *superscription* to Psalm 18 provides an interesting case in point. This poem is also preserved in 2 Samuel 22 in a specific historical setting. That setting is recalled in the psalm's superscription. However, Psalm 18 has now been placed in the Psalter in which David is understood as a representative rather than unique person; and, indeed, Psalm 17, an individual lament, precedes this psalm. In this way, the placement of Psalm 18 has helped make possible a broader interpretation of the text, one beyond the specific setting in David's experience and one applicable to the community's pilgrimage of faith.

Rhetoric

A final matter of concern when interpreting the royal psalms is their rhetoric. These texts embody quite a diversity of form, and the framework in which their rhetoric functions depends on the form. In each case, however, the primary issue is the success of the king. In the psalms referring to battle, the question is whether God will grant victory to the Davidic king and thus to the people. The issue in other royal psalms, especially those related to the king's coronation, is whether the monarch will live up to the royal ideal. In such a setting, the rhetoric of these psalms heightens these concerns for king and community and instills hope that God will remain faithful to the kingdom.

The images that these texts use thus often relate to the king—as victor, as the one whom God has honored, as the defender of the faith and the powerless—who represents the faithful God who has guaranteed the king's rule. The repetition in the psalms also often centers on the unique role of the king. Because the king is God's representative, he has a special relationship with God. The king becomes Yahweh's adopted son (Ps 2:7), the Davidic king to whom Yahweh has sworn a sure oath (Ps 132:11) that he and his line will rule as Yahweh's representatives over the people in Jerusalem. Because of the king's special relationship, the royal psalms also reflect a willingness to ask Yahweh for help. At this point, the appearance of traditional language from ancient Israel's faith becomes strategic. The king, as in Psalms 72 and 101, is to be the "righteous guarantor of justice," loaded terms in ancient Israel's faith; but the promise to the king has also become a central tenet in the community's theology. The Davidic covenant (2 Sam 7) forms much of the backdrop to these texts. Especially in Psalm 89, the appeal for help is based on that covenant tradition. Yahweh graciously made a promise to David and his line that they would rule over the people in Jerusalem as God's chosen representatives. In this royal lament, that promise is in jeopardy, and the speaker appeals for Yahweh to keep that promise. Psalm 18 celebrates Yahweh's faithfulness to that covenant promise. The promise holds relevance for the community as well, because the righteous king is the channel for blessing to the people. Thus ancient Israel's faith tradition is an integral part of these psalms. The rhetoric of the royal psalms brings the ruler's pilgrimage into the public life of the community and considers it in light of God's promise of faithfulness. A look at three representative royal psalms should further our understanding of these texts.

Three Royal Psalms

(1) Psalm 2 is the first of the royal psalms. The first of four sections describes the plotting of rebellious vassals. Note the parallelism.

> Why do the nations conspire,
>   and the peoples plot in vain?
> The kings of the earth set themselves,
>   and the rulers take counsel together,
>   against the LORD and his anointed, saying,
> "Let us burst their bonds asunder,
>   and cast their cords from us." (vv. 1-3)

The next section describes, in no uncertain terms, God's response to such a prospect.

> He who sits in the heavens laughs;
>   the LORD has them in derision.
> Then he will speak to them in his wrath,
>   and terrify them in his fury, saying,
> "I have set my king
>   on Zion, my holy hill." (vv. 4-6)

The following verses portray the king as the speaker of Yahweh's decree concerning the throne.

> I will tell of the decree of the LORD:
> He said to me, "You are my son,
>   today I have begotten you.
> Ask of me, and I will make the nations your heritage,
>   and the ends of the earth your possession.
> You shall break them in pieces like a potter's vessel."
>   (vv. 7-9)

The psalm concludes with a call to the "rulers of the earth" to submit to Yahweh's authority.

> Now therefore, O kings, be wise;
>   be warned, O rulers of the earth.
> Serve the LORD with fear,
>   with trembling kiss his feet,
> lest he be angry, and you perish in the way;
>   for his wrath is quickly kindled.
> Blessed are all who take refuge in him. (vv. 10-12)

This text likely came from a ritual related to the coronation of the king; at such a vulnerable time, this psalm would declare God's commitment to the monarch and God's guarantee of the Davidic rule.

The psalm appears at the beginning of the Psalter and is related to Psalm 1; our text calls for the same decision between the life that Yahweh offers and that which the wicked offer. The conclusion of Psalm 2 calls nations to make the wise decision for life found with Yahweh. The placement of the psalm already, then, indicates that the text has been shaped in such a way that it has a broader application to the life of faith and does not relate only to the coronation of a Davidic king in pre-exilic Jerusalem. The text has through the centuries offered communities of faith the sure hope of the coming kingdom of God. The structure of the psalm supports this view. The first and last sections speak of Yahweh's authority, and the second and third sections of God's choice of the Davidic monarch as the divine representative. God's response to rebellion is firm! The Davidic choice and covenant stand. The picture of rebellion and God's response in laughter and fury offer a powerful reminder that God is the giver of life. Also worthy of note is the king's use of the scepter to smash a pot (v. 9); this is the fate of rebels. Psalm 2, then, vividly calls nations to the reality that Yahweh, with Yahweh's Davidic representative, is the authoritative giver of life.

(2) *Psalm 101* further contributes to our picture of the royal ideal in ancient Israel. Along with the privilege of rule comes responsibility. Psalm 72 prays that the king will be just; Psalm 101 recounts the king's pledge to fulfill that ideal. The psalm was also probably part of the coronation ceremonies, or their anniversary, and is a kind of "oath of office" by the king. While the text does not actually mention the king, it is plain that the speaker is the leader of the community, and the psalm offers assurance that the leader will be loyal to the royal ideal. The lack of mention of the king does, however, facilitate a broader application of the text to community leaders and all persons of faith; thus faith communities still make use of this poem.

The rhetoric of the text is powerful and pointed. The oath that the king takes is active and part of a close relationship with Yahweh; note the frequent use of "I" as the king speaks to Yahweh

in the form of direct address. The psalm makes use of the divine
name only in the first and last verses.

> I will sing of loyalty and of justice;
>> to thee, O LORD, I will sing.
> I will give heed to the way that is blameless.
>> Oh when wilt thou come to me?
> I will walk with integrity of heart
>> within my house;
> I will not set before my eyes
>> anything that is base.
> I hate the work of those who fall away;
>> it shall not cleave to me.
> Perverseness of heart shall be far from me;
>> I will know nothing of evil.
> Him who slanders his neighbor secretly
>> I will destroy.
> The man of haughty looks and arrogant heart
>> I will not endure.
> I will look with favor on the faithful in the land,
>> that they may dwell with me;
> he who walks in the way that is blameless
>> shall minister to me.
> No man who practices deceit
>> shall dwell in my house;
> no man who utters lies
>> shall continue in my presence.
> Morning by morning I will destroy
>> all the wicked in the land,
> cutting off all the evildoers
>> from the city of the LORD. (Ps 101)

The king pledges an upright life (walk in his house) and rule.
The psalm is replete with images of lifestyle, and in this case, the
king pledges to guarantee the blessing of the faithful lifestyle. The
king is the guarantor of justice in the kingdom, and the traditional terms of ancient Israel's faith (justice, integrity, the faithful) infuse the royal ideal. Verses 1 and 2 speak of the positive
pledge of the king, and vv. 3–5 of that which he rejects. In like
manner, v. 6 speaks of a positive lifestyle, and vv. 7 and 8 the
opposing way of life. This latter part of the psalm uses "the echo

effect" with great success. The rhetoric of Psalm 101 demonstrates ancient Israel's high expectations of the community leader.

(3) *Psalm 132* gives a further indication of the power of the Davidic monarchy. This text also probably arises from a setting that reenacts and celebrates the divine choice of the Davidic line to rule on Zion (v. 11). The first part of the psalm describes David's attempt to bring the ark of the covenant to Jerusalem as a symbol of God's presence there. The section concludes with a reminder of the promise to David. The last part of the psalm celebrates Yahweh's choice of Zion as the place of divine presence and blessing. The psalm thus moves through Davidic faithfulness, divine promise, and blessing. The language of the text centers on the blessing presence of Yahweh, a blessing initially tied to the divine kingdom but one that later came to center in the community. As a result, people of faith have throughout the centuries been able to claim the power of this text for the contemporary life of faith. Readers of Psalm 132 continue, as in ancient Israel, to live between the promise of Yahweh's kingdom and its realization.

The psalm begins with the vivid memory of David's search for the ark.

> Remember, O LORD, in David's favor,
>   all the hardships he endured;
> how he swore to the LORD
>   and vowed to the Mighty One of Jacob,
> "I will not enter my house
>   or get into my bed;
> I will not give sleep to my eyes
>   or slumber to my eyelids,
> until I find a place for the LORD,
>   a dwelling place for the Mighty One of Jacob."
>   (vv. 1–5)

Will David fulfill the royal ideal?

> Lo, we heard of it in Ephrathah,
>   we found it in the fields of Jaar.
> "Let us go to his dwelling place;
>   let us worship at his footstool!" (vv. 6, 7)

Verses 8–10 are reminiscent of the ark narratives in Numbers (10:35, 36), when the ark led the people into battle as they progressed toward the promised land. In Psalm 132, these words relate to the divine presence on Zion and the blessing for the community and the Davidic line occasioned by that presence.

> Arise, O LORD, and go to thy resting place,
>   thou and the ark of thy might.
> Let thy priests be clothed with righteousness,
>   and let thy saints shout for joy.
> For thy servant David's sake
>   do not turn away the face of thy anointed one.

Verses 1–10 are actually a petition that Yahweh remember David's strenuous and faithful efforts and thus "clothe" the priests in righteousness and grant the king victory. A righteous royal establishment assures blessing for the people. Verses 11 and 12 speak specifically of Nathan's promise (2 Sam 7), or the Davidic covenant promise, that David and his line would represent Yahweh in ruling over the people in Jerusalem. The repetition of the promise offers assurance and, in this case, also calls the king to covenant obedience.

> The LORD swore to David a sure oath
>   from which he will not turn back:
> "One of the sons of your body
>   I will set on your throne.
> If your sons keep my covenant
>   and my testimonies which I shall teach them,
> their sons also for ever
>   shall sit upon your throne." (vv. 11, 12)

The remainder of the text ties the choice of the Davidic line with the choice of Zion as the divine dwelling or "resting place" (v. 8). From Zion comes blessing and protection for the community, including the poor (v. 15), and victory for the king. This last section of the psalm (vv. 13–18) demonstrates the special relation the monarch has with Yahweh. It also quotes Yahweh as it had in vv. 11 and 12; the first part of the psalm quotes David. Verses 13–18 remind the reader of vv. 1–5. Matching lines predominate in both sections. Note the contrast in the psalm's concluding verse.

> For the LORD has chosen Zion;
>   he has desired it for his habitation:
> "This is my resting place for ever;
>   here I will dwell, for I have desired it.
> I will abundantly bless her provisions;
>   I will satisfy her poor with bread.
> Her priests I will clothe with salvation,
>   and her saints will shout for joy.
> There I will make a horn to sprout for David;
>   I have prepared a lamp for my anointed.
> His enemies I will clothe with shame,
>   but upon himself his crown will shed its luster."

The Davidic effort and covenant as well as the divine choice of Zion provide, in this prayer, motivation for divine favor for the royal-Zion establishment.

Conclusion

While the royal psalms may not be numerous, they were central for ancient Israel because they spoke of a foremost way in which the God of Zion was active among the people—by way of the Davidic monarchy. The monarch could be the channel of blessing for the community, and his rule is clearly related to the divine presence in Zion. These texts, therefore, hold import for the community that sought divine sanction and power.

These psalms describe the king as God's representative ruling over the kingdom that God has established. The texts likewise speak of the promise of the dominion of Yahweh over all. The Davidic kingdom was one historical expression of that dominion, and these texts look backward to it. The texts, however, often look forward to the fulfillment of the ideal of the Davidic kingdom. In that sense the texts are forward looking as were their readers. Subsequent readers also live between the promised kingdom of God and its consummation. For later readers, these texts offer hope and encouragement for faith. As the community recites these psalms, it articulates and strengthens a significant aspect of its faith and hope. So the royal psalms are of theological, as well as historical, import. The texts picture Yahweh as "king," a term that may be offensive to some. Readers might find the phrase "giver of life" to be more constructive.

This chapter has treated texts pertaining to the life of the Davidic king. They come from a variety of settings and take a variety of forms. These texts also relate to blessing for the community and thus have meaning beyond their original setting. The relationship between Yahweh and the king and this relationship's tie to blessing for the community are important aspects of the Old Testament book of Psalms. One final category of the Psalter needs our attention—wisdom psalms.

Wisdom Psalms:
I Will Instruct You

7

As with the royal psalms, scholars have debated whether the category "wisdom psalms" is appropriate for a class of psalms. These texts do, however, exhibit a form and origin that differ from other psalms and thus require separate treatment. The psalms in the chart below also have common characteristics, which affords further reason for treating them as a group.

WISDOM PSALMS			
1	49	112	128
32	73	119	133
37	78	127	

The category "wisdom psalms" is appropriate because of the origins of the psalms. These texts originated among ancient Israel's wisdom circles, who sought to pass on wisdom for living; their purpose for future generations was one of teaching/ warning.[1] Wisdom seeks, through the teacher/learner relationship, to pass on what the teachers have discovered about the way of life that God has created. The wise find this way of

---

[1]See Anderson, *Out of the Depths*, 215–27.

life and live by it. The wisdom psalms give instruction for living and thus reflect the function of the wisdom circles.

These psalms also contain many of the forms characteristic of wisdom texts:

1. The better saying:
   Better is a little that the righteous has
   than the abundance of many wicked. (Ps 37:16)

2. The blessed saying:
   Blessed is every one who fears the LORD,
   who walks in his ways! (Ps 128:1)

3. The warning:
   Be not like a horse or a mule, without
   understanding,
   which must be curbed with bit and bridle,
   else it will not keep with you. (Ps 32:9)

4. The address:
   Hear this, all peoples!
   Give ear, all inhabitants of the world,
   both low and high,
   rich and poor together! (Ps 49:1, 2)

5. Other forms characteristic of wisdom such as the simile, numerical saying, or rhetorical question:
   The wicked are not so,
   but are like chaff which the wind drives away.
   (Ps 1:4)

These psalms also reflect many of the themes common to ancient Israel's wisdom literature:

1. The fear of Yahweh and the love of "torah." Psalm 119 is an extended meditation on this topic.
2. The contrast between righteous and wicked. These terms reflect two lifestyles which bring blessing or suffering respectively. Such a view brings the problem of the prosperity of the wicked to the fore. Psalms 49, 73, 112, and 127 deal with such topics.[2]

---

[2]The topic of theodicy—how one accounts for the justice of God in the face of evil—has continued to be a major concern for the community of faith, even to the present.

3. Instruction in daily living. Psalm 133 fits this category as does Psalm 112:5:

It is well with the man who deals generously
    and lends,
who conducts his affairs with justice.

Wisdom teachers often addressed the future generation as "my son," which has led some to conclude that wisdom texts may have originally come from a setting of family instruction. But a number of other scholars suggest that teachers passed on wisdom in schools associated with the royal court. Texts like these provided guidance and instruction for living a full life; they helped develop skill in living the wise life. As we would expect with texts coming from such a setting, the psalms have an optimistic view of life.

Wisdom texts such as Proverbs, Job, and Ecclesiastes are informed by a creation theology. God created the world and life and placed in it wisdom. The creator enables persons to discover, through observation, this wisdom and to live by it. Wisdom teachers would pass on this education for living, or wisdom, which was to result in fullness of life for those who live by it. The wisdom psalms arose from this kind of background and, using forms appropriate to the teaching task, sought to nurture the wise life among members of the faith community, which likely made use of the texts in family settings and public settings such as the synagogue.

The Texts

Information on the background of the wisdom psalms should facilitate our brief survey of these texts. Psalm 1 presents a stark contrast between the life of the righteous and the wicked and remarks on the consequences of life's choices. The psalm seeks to encourage the individual to choose righteousness. The contrast between righteous and wicked is central to a number of wisdom psalms.

Psalm 49 begins with a reference to the forms and task of wisdom and proceeds to the problem of the prosperity of the wicked. The wicked will also die; retribution is inevitable for them. The text serves as a brief meditation on the meaning of life. The psalm affirms that all perish:

> Man cannot abide in his pomp,
>   he is like the beasts that perish. (v. 20)

The central figures, however, are the rich who come to the same inevitable end:

> For when he dies he will carry nothing away;
>   his glory will not go down after him. (v. 17)

Psalm 112 reflects a similar view that retribution for the wicked is inevitable, but this text concentrates on the blessing for the wise, those who "fear the LORD" (v. 1). The wise receive wealth and riches and family blessings. They also contribute generously to the community, receiving a manifold return for their generosity. Psalms 127 and 128 also emphasize the blessings of the life of faith. The first of these texts points to the blessing of children:

> Like arrows in the hand of a warrior
>   are the sons of one's youth. (v. 4)

The fullness of blessing for the righteous is put in no uncertain terms in the first two verses of Psalm 128:

> Blessed is every one who fears the LORD,
>   who walks in his ways!
> You shall eat the fruit of the labor of your hands;
>   you shall be happy, and it shall be well with you.

Psalm 73 deals with this same issue of the contrast between righteous and wicked but perhaps at a more profound level. The view that the righteous are rewarded and the wicked punished raised questions when the speaker considered the prosperity of the wicked.

> Truly God is good to the upright,
>   to those who are pure in heart.
> But as for me, my feet had almost stumbled,
>   my steps had well nigh slipped.
> For I was envious of the arrogant,
>   when I saw the prosperity of the wicked. (vv. 1–3)

The psalm describes the dilemma, and only in the context of worship (vv. 16, 17) did the person come to the conclusion that life has a moral order. This experience brought profound gratitude (v. 28).

Psalms 32 and 37 reflect a similar view of the contrast between righteous and wicked but in the context of instruction. Using a proverbial form, Psalm 32 instructs the righteous to confess sin to God and to seek forgiveness; God will grant forgiveness and the blessing of a full life.

> Many are the pangs of the wicked;
>   but steadfast love surrounds him who trusts in the
>   LORD. (v. 10)

Similar in form and content to the book of Proverbs, Psalm 37 instructs in the life of righteousness and assures readers/hearers that it reaps great reward. The psalm inculcates righteous living in the community. The psalm's first four verses well embody its message:

> Fret not yourself because of the wicked,
>   be not envious of wrongdoers!
> For they will soon fade like the grass,
>   and wither like the green herb.
> Trust in the LORD, and do good;
>   so you will dwell in the land, and enjoy security.
> Take delight in the LORD,
>   and he will give you the desires of your heart.

The brief Psalm 133 rejoices in the blessing of unity within the community and interprets this blessing as the result of righteous living. Several of the wisdom psalms, then, begin with a strong contrast between the righteous and the wicked in order to nurture the life of righteousness in the faith community.

Psalm 119 takes a similar view of the issue but pursues other directions. This text is the longest in the Psalter and is an extended meditation on the "torah" of Yahweh. The psalm is an alphabetic acrostic, another form characteristic of wisdom texts. In this acrostic each stanza begins with a successive letter in the Hebrew alphabet. The psalm celebrates in many ways the instruction that God gives for life. The speaker seeks instruction in Yahweh's statutes, because obedience to that wisdom constitutes "the fear (reverence) of the LORD," and therein is found blessing in life. The speaker earnestly yearns for God's blessing and displays loyalty to God's wisdom.

> Oh, how I love thy law!
> It is my meditation all the day.
> Thy commandment makes me wiser than my enemies,
> for it is ever with me. (vv. 97, 98)

Psalm 78 is a rather different wisdom psalm. The text begins with reference to common wisdom features: the desire to teach, the use of parables, and the purpose of passing on traditions to future generations. The poem next emphasizes the teaching function of the torah, as do other wisdom psalms, in order to promote faithfulness to that torah. The remainder of the text recounts the history of God's gracious provision for the people and the continuing sin of Ephraim even in the face of blessing. Because of Israel's sin, Yahweh chose Judah and the Davidic house and guided them and blessed them. The psalm thus gives a rationale for Yahweh's choice of Judah rather than the kingdom of Israel (Ephraim), but it also warns future generations to avoid rejection because of disobedience. So while this text is a bit different and more historical in orientation, it still instructs and encourages wisdom and righteousness, and functions in line with other wisdom psalms.

Shaping and Rhetoric

Our look at the texts of the wisdom psalms should help us consider the forces at work as these poems became part of the Psalter. (1) Of particular importance is the *organization of the Psalter.* Psalm 1 introduces the Psalter and sets the tone of the collection in terms of the choice between the life of the righteous and the wicked. In addition, with its reference to Yahweh's instruction (v. 2), it directs the faith community to view the Psalter as teaching about the life of faith. The instruction in the Psalms centers on the honest dialogue between creator and the created that is at the heart of the life of faith. Placing this wisdom psalm as the introduction to the Psalter helps readers view the Psalms as having significance for the life of faith beyond the texts' original cultic setting. Also worthy of note is the fact that other kinds of psalms include wisdom elements (e.g., Pss 14; 26; 36) that allow the community to apply these texts broadly to the pilgrimage of faith. Wisdom texts, then, are integral in determining the final shape of the Psalter.

(2) Related to this first concern is the *language of the Psalter*. When Psalms 49 and 73 deal with the issue of reward for the righteous and retribution for the wicked, the language does not bind these psalms to a single original setting; the language is instead adaptable to a range of settings in life. Indeed, the instructive purposes of the texts reflect a larger *community emphasis*. The purpose of recounting personal experience (Ps 73) or history (Ps 78) is to pass on wisdom for the faith community. These texts offer hope to that community, hope that the life of faith is worth the effort.

The rhetoric of the wisdom psalms also has a profound impact on the reader. These texts do not display the kind of common literary form of the hymns or laments, but their desire to nurture the righteous life appears to surface in their rhetoric contrasting the righteous and the wicked. A concern for righteous, or "wise," living is present in all these psalms; we noted examples above. The beginning of Psalm 73 reflects the theme.

> Truly God is good to the upright,
>   to those who are pure in heart. (v. 1)

The psalm also draws the contrast later with a reference to the wicked.

> Truly thou dost set them in slippery places;
>   thou dost make them fall to ruin. (v. 18)

The repeated contrast, often by way of striking antithetic parallelism, highlights the psalm's message. The structure of Psalm 1 hinges on the contrast. The concluding verse of that psalm also shows how the contrast closely relates to Yahweh's intention.

for the LORD knows the way of the righteous,
    but the way of the wicked will perish. (v. 6)

The imagery in these psalms reinforces the contrast, especially when it comes to the fate of the righteous and wicked. On the one hand, the wicked will be cut off and wither, often by way of their own evil.

The wicked draw the sword and bend their bows,
    to bring down the poor and needy,
    to slay those who walk uprightly;
their sword shall enter their own heart,
    and their bows shall be broken. (Ps 37:14, 15)

The righteous, on the other hand, prosper and grow luxuriantly.

Blessed is every one who fears the LORD,
    who walks in his ways!
You shall eat the fruit of the labor of your hands;
    you shall be happy, and it shall be well with you.
Your wife will be like a fruitful vine within your house;
    your children will be like olive shoots around your
        table.
Lo, thus shall the man be blessed
    who fears the LORD. (Ps 128:1-4)

The fear of the Lord brings to mind Old Testament wisdom passages (e.g., Prov 1:7)[3] and reminds us that these texts use traditional terms from ancient Israel's faith to describe the righteous as people of faith—as over against the wicked who have no faith. As a means of nurturing righteousness in the faith community, these texts tend to affirm the traditional doctrine of reward and retribution: one finds reward in righteous living and trouble in evil.

Many are the pangs of the wicked;
    but steadfast love surrounds him who trusts in the
        LORD. (Ps 32:10)

---

[3]Note in Prov 1:7 the use of the feminine חָכְמָה (*ḥokmâ*), "wisdom." Proverbs also employs the image of Woman Wisdom in descriptions of Yahweh as the one who reveals wisdom.

Two Wisdom Psalms

Our study of the wisdom psalms will be benefited by a look at some of the aspects involved in interpreting two passages, Psalms 1 and 37.

(1) Psalm 1 is the first of the wisdom texts. It describes two basic lifestyles, that of the righteous and that of the wicked. The psalm's structure accentuates the contrast or antithesis between the two ways of life. The first part of the text describes the righteous life, its guide (torah) in relation to God, and its results.

> Blessed is the man
> who walks not in the counsel of the wicked,
> nor stands in the way of sinners,
>   nor sits in the seat of scoffers;
> but his delight is in the law of the LORD,
>   and on his law he meditates day and night.
> He is like a tree
>   planted by streams of water,
> that yields its fruit in its seasons,
>   and its leaf does not wither.
> In all that he does, he prospers. (vv. 1–3)

The fate of the wicked contrasts starkly.

> The wicked are not so,
>   but are like chaff which the wind drives away.
> Therefore the wicked will not stand in the judgment,
>   nor sinners in the congregation of the righteous;
> for the LORD knows the way of the righteous,
>   but the way of the wicked will perish. (vv. 4–6)

The form (beatitude) and content of the psalm are reflective of popular royal wisdom in the Old Testament. The text seeks to pass on wisdom concerning the basic structure of life with traditional terms of the faith: wicked, sinners, law, judgment, righteous. The righteous life has a relationship with Yahweh and results in prosperity. Note the image of the tree that is deeply rooted and yields fruit and prospers. In contrast are the wicked, like chaff blown away, with no place in the congregation; their way perishes. This contrast between the two lifestyles is at the heart of the psalm. Its rhetoric calls persons to choose between the two styles of life and to choose righteousness, the way of wholeness, the way of Yahweh. The choice determines life or death, and so the text educates in the right orientation of life. We have already seen the part Psalm 1 plays as introduction to the Psalter; its language also gives it a universal dimension. Its content is instructive for communities beyond ancient Israel.

(2) *Psalm 37* also reflects many features of wisdom literature. It is similar to Proverbs in many ways and concentrates on the contrast between the righteous and the wicked. The text also reflects a background in popular royal wisdom with its desire to teach or to pass on wisdom for the proper orientation in life. The acrostic form of the text may also be a teaching, memory device. The psalm's rhetoric concentrates on the distinction between the righteous and the wicked and uses traditional terms in so doing. The life of righteousness, fear of God, trust in God, and reward are contrasted, often by way of antithetic parallelism, with the life of evil and retribution.

> For the arms of the wicked shall be broken;
>   but the LORD upholds the righteous. . . .
> The mouth of the righteous utters wisdom,
>   and his tongue speaks justice.
> The law of his God is in his heart;
>   his steps do not slip. . . .
> The LORD helps them and delivers them;
>   he delivers them from the wicked, and saves them,
>   because they take refuge in him. (vv. 17, 30, 31, 40)

The text thus reaches its climax (vv. 39, 40) by emphasizing that the righteous belong to Yahweh. Indeed, reward for the righteous includes prosperity in the land.

> Yet a little while, and the wicked will be no more;
>   though you look well at his place, he will not be
>   there.
> But the meek shall possess the land,
>   and delight themselves in abundant prosperity.
>   (vv. 10, 11)

Note also vv. 9, 14, 15, 18, 20–22, 29, 38. The psalm fosters the life of righteousness and speaks universally to the structure of life as Yahweh created it. People of faith in every generation can, because its language is so adaptable, grow from the study of Psalm 37.

This chapter has considered the wisdom psalms and their background and function. The chapter should complete our picture of the different types of psalms and the different methods involved in interpreting them. The concluding chapter will bring together a number of these concerns in terms of the major theological themes in the Book of Praises.

The Psalms and Faith

8

One might describe the Psalter as the beginnings of theology, for in these texts the faith community, ancient Israel, recalled its life experiences in relation to its faith tradition and sought to integrate the two, thereby making theological sense out of experience. At the same time, in part because of the nature of theologizing and in part because of the great diversity involved, scholars have always found difficulty in speaking of a theology of the Psalms. The book is not a systematic presentation of theological constructs, but it is fundamentally theological. This concluding chapter will thus describe eight theological themes in the Psalter. The themes have arisen from our consideration of these texts and should provide an opportunity to reflect on our overall journey through the Psalms.

The Honest Dialogue of Faith

Psalm 1 is a good starting point for our discussion. In the last chapter, we saw how those who shaped the Psalter have placed this text at the beginning of the book as an introduction. Many students of the Psalms have noted this fact but have seldom commented on its significance. As an introduction, Psalm 1 shifts the function of the book of Psalms from being primarily

a response to God to being a revelation from God.[1] This part of
the shaping of the Psalter presents the collection of texts to follow
as part of God's "torah" upon which the faithful are called to
meditate as a guide for the life of faith.

> Blessed is the man
> who walks not in the counsel of the wicked,
> nor stands in the way of sinners,
>   nor sits in the seat of scoffers;
> but his delight is in the law of the LORD,
>   and on his law he meditates day and night. (vv. 1, 2)

Since the Psalter is essentially addressed to God as prayer,
its instruction concerns the honest dialogue at the center of the
life of faith. The Psalms give guidance by example in how to con-
verse with God in the midst of life, and this instruction in dialogue relates to every human condition. It portrays praise in the
midst of joy and complaint in the midst of pain. Thus the Psalter
offers instruction for the journey of faith and recounts the dialogue with God that is at the heart of that journey. From its out-
set in Psalm 1, this dialogue traverses the pilgrimage of faith and
ends in the uninhibited praise of God in Psalm 150, a sign that
the faith journey is satisfying. Note the similar theme in Psalm
1:3 with reference to the righteous person:

> He is like a tree
>   planted by streams of water,
> that yields its fruit in its season,
>   and its leaf does not wither.
> In all that he does, he prospers.

The last line of Psalm 2 affirms the same reality for nations.

At the beginning of our study, we came to see the Psalms
as pilgrimage songs of faith, songs that furnish insight and encouragement for the journey of faith. The shape of the Psalter
confirms that view. We now consider various aspects of the
Psalter's torah or instruction for the faith journey.

---

[1]See Childs, *Introduction*, 513–14.

Worship

Worship, a key feature of the book of Psalms, is the act in which the community celebrates and thereby makes available God's presence and activity. Thus the Psalms' portrayal of worship begins with divine presence and activity rather than with human initiative. This perspective on worship is characteristic of biblical theology. Worship is a corporate response to divine presence and activity, and it is also an arena for divine action. The purpose of worship, the encounter between God and community, is to bring renewal for full, obedient living. The Psalms' portrayal of worship includes a variety of elements: praise, confession, proclamation, commitment. As such, worship in the Psalms is not passive but active.

Psalms 46 and 48, Zion psalms, illustrate how the Psalter celebrates the divine presence in worship. The sanctuary as the place of the divine presence from which flows the sustaining and renewing river of life forms the background for worship (Pss 46:4, 5; 48:10). Because worship celebrates God's renewing presence in Zion and in the community, the Psalms, like Psalm 84, also display a yearning for this experience.

> My soul longs, yea, faints
>   for the courts of the LORD;
> my heart and flesh sing for joy
>   to the living God. (84:2)

Psalms 15 and 24 similarly reflect this exuberance for worship. These psalms, along with others such as Psalm 95, emphasize the prophetic view that worship is closely related to ethical living.

In addition to the celebration of the divine presence, the Psalms also recount in worship the history of God's saving activity. The community remembers its history in order to make it relevant for the present. Psalms 68 and 105 recount salvation history so that the current congregation will recognize that it is part of that continuing history; God is still the God who delivers. Witness the contemporary description of God in the conclusion of Psalm 68 or Psalm 105:4:

Seek the LORD and his strength,
seek his presence continually!

The worshipers reenacted their history in a dramatic fashion to facilitate the divine-human encounter and thus encourage faith for living.

Praise

The theme of worship pervades the Psalter, and one of the main elements of worship is praise. One of the basic categories in our classification of the Psalms is the hymns of praise. We have already observed that their typical structure suggests several dimensions of praise. First, praise is always substantive; the body of these psalms of praise gives reasons for praising God: God's saving activity, God's instruction, the divine presence. Second, the Psalms enact the praise of God by recounting God's presence and activity rather than by fabricating emotional displays. Third, the praise of God in the Psalms is honest; it is genuine and uninhibited.

Praise, as worship, begins with God's involvement on behalf of the community. Many of the reasons psalms give for praising God relate to God's loyalty to the people and the constant divine effort to create life for them (Pss 117; 122; 134). The community gathers and praises God in response to such grace, a response from gratitude and need and hope. The Psalms also praise Yahweh as the sovereign creator who brings order and life out of chaos. Psalms 98 and 150 reflect this view. The concluding psalm in the Psalter is a universal call to praise God because of the joy found in a life bound up with praise. The Psalms understand life as gift from God. The full exercise of that gift requires worship and praise, both central aspects to the Psalter. The divine-human encounter in praise and worship brings renewal for the journey of faith.[2]

---

[2]See J. Durham, "Psalms," *Broadman Bible Commentary* (Nashville: Broadman Press, 1971) 4:167-70.

Pain

Our concerns with praise and worship center on the psalms of praise that speak of the presence of God. The laments speak of the absence of God, an important dimension of the honest dialogue of faith. The Psalms' portrayal of pain holds many dimensions, but let us consider the topic first from the divine perspective and then from the human side.

Central to ancient Israel's faith was the Exodus experience. In the honest dialogue of faith that was part of those events, the community expressed anguish and sought God's help. Yahweh embraced their pain. Jacob/Israel sought healing from God, and that is what the congregation sought in the lament psalms. Expressions of pain were woven into their worship experience. The structure of the laments also affords valuable insight at this point in that laments typically end with a positive tone as an indication of some resolution to the pain. God has become involved in the journey toward healing. The laments make clear that expressing pain is part of the Psalms' honest dialogue of faith. Texts like these help the community acknowledge the suffering encountered in life and express that pain. That kind of expression is a necessary prerequisite to moving through the hardship. Texts like Psalm 88, the most despairing in the Psalter, help make possible the pilgrimage through anguish to hope. Laments give form to the pain and grief of life.

> O LORD, my God, I call for help by day;
>   I cry out in the night before thee.
> Let my prayer come before thee,
>   incline thy ear to my cry!
> For my soul is full of troubles,
>   and my life draws near to Sheol. (vv. 1–3)

The laments often speak of pain in terms of being gripped by the power of death or of a sojourn in the jaws of death. The manifestation of the power of death may result from injustice, as in Psalm 7 or Psalm 109:

> Be not silent, O God of my praise!
> For wicked and deceitful mouths are opened against
>   me,
>   speaking against me with lying tongues. (vv. 1, 2)

This text expresses its anguish in brutal honesty and pleads for God's deliverance and just judgment of the enemies. The hiding of the face of God may also bring despair. Psalm 27:9 pleads, "Hide not thy face from me." The laments cry to Yahweh for help, and the divine absence/presence becomes a pressing issue in the midst of crisis. Psalm 22 begins with that issue:

> My God, my God, why hast thou forsaken me?
>   Why art thou so far from helping me, from the words
>   of my groaning?
> O my God, I cry by day, but thou dost not answer;
>   and by night, but find no rest. (vv. 1, 2)

The speaker functions in a context of faith, and the text continues by honestly expressing great anguish. The conclusion of the psalm indicates that the tension between faith in the God who delivers and the experience of pain has been resolved. Just as the psalm expresses despair honestly, it also offers exuberant praise to the God who delivers. This text is a good illustration of the fact that the speakers of laments are theologizing, seeking to make sense out of their faith tradition in the face of their experience of affliction. To acknowledge and express hurt is a risk, but the Psalms affirm the possibility of newness in so doing. So the laments bear witness to the journey through pain and its expression to the hope found in the conclusions of many of these psalms.

Hope

Our discussion of the Psalms' expression of despair leads to the recognition of hope in these texts. The laments often express hope in striking ways as they come to a positive conclusion, even in the face of a momentous crisis. The worshipers based their hope on God's involvement in life. Praying the laments then constituted an act of hope. Psalm 130 illustrates this with its call for the congregation to "hope in the LORD" (v. 7), while emerging from the darkness of human despair: "Out of the depths I cry to thee, O LORD!" (v. 1).

The Psalms express hope in a variety of ways. The laments move from despair to hope. Psalm 6 is interrupted after v. 7 and suddenly moves to an affirmation of God's involvement in life. Perhaps in the context of worship there was a word of hope which engendered the move from death and the Pit to the shelter of the wings. Psalms 57 and 61 describe the shelter of God's presence with the image of safety under the wings. Safety promised by God brings hope and the possibility of newness in life. Note the association of the sanctuary with hope. The Psalms also associate hope with the faith community; there one encounters hope, hope firmly based in the faith tradition that demonstrates God's trustworthiness (Pss 11; 42–43). So the Psalms raise the issue of hope even in the face of pain, and hope can lead one through hardship and trial. The Psalms are honest pilgrimage songs of faith and thus deal with all of life, including despair and hope. Hope is not always at hand, but the Psalms persevere in the journey through crisis toward hope's light and liberation.

Hope is a major theme in both the absence and the presence of God. The creation and enthronement psalms affirm that God has created and continues to sustain the creation. This issues in a universal hope for meaning and order in life, such as we see in Psalm 8 and Psalm 139. In the Psalter, hope centers in the powerful encounter with Yahweh.

Justice

Readers of the Psalms so often concentrate on aspects of prayer and worship in these texts that they miss the theme of justice which is distinctly present in the Psalms. The reader may easily get an unbalanced view of the Psalter by thinking that topics like social justice and oppression belong only to the Prophets, but these themes are also important in Old Testament worship literature.

The Psalms are anything but bland. They speak about life in concrete and immediate terms, perhaps even raw and earthy terms. Because the Psalms are often brutally honest we should not expect them to ignore one of the hard realities of the human experience, injustice. We have already seen that honest cries for justice in the Psalter are passionate acts of hope because they hinge on God's involvement in the face of injustice and oppression. The Psalms seek righteousness and justice for the oppressed, and sometimes do so in ways that make readers uncomfortable. Students of the Psalms need to remember, however, that these prayers were spoken in the context of worship. Even the cries for vengeance, which are really cries for justice—cries which beg God to show that the life of faith makes sense—are prayers. The worshipers prayed for God to bring about justice, which would enable them to integrate their faith tradition with the harsh realities of life. Some of the prayers express anger to Yahweh, the God of justice, the God who supports faith and righteousness and opposes evil. The worshipers yearn for a demonstration of justice so that life could again have significance. Psalm 17 pleads for justice in the face of accusation and concludes with trust in the God of justice.

> Hear a just cause, O LORD; attend to my cry!
>   Give ear to my prayer from lips free of deceit!
> From thee let my vindication come!
>   Let thy eyes see the right! (vv. 1, 2)

In like manner, Psalm 26 calls for an affirmation of integrity from the God of unchanging loyalty. Psalm 74 cries for justice for a fallen Jerusalem, justice in the midst of great affliction. This psalm also seeks a demonstration of Yahweh's unchanging love.

In our look at the royal psalms, we noted that the monarch was to be the guarantor of justice. This was the ruler's primary function. Psalm 72 prays that the king will be just and bring liberation for the oppressed and a life of equality among covenant brothers and sisters. Justice is a primary theme in the Psalter.

Community

Because individualism predominates the perspective of contemporary Western society, many readers find the Old Testament emphasis on a corporate community difficult to comprehend. The community is essential for the Psalms' basic notions of life and death. Inclusion in the community is prerequisite for life. Therefore, the first point of reference for the Psalms is not the individual but the community, specifically the community of faith, because the faith is a shared tradition. The individual finds life and hope in community.

Psalm 1 shows that people live and grow in community and choose between two types of community for guidance—either the righteous or the wicked.

> Blessed is the man
> who walks not in the counsel of the wicked,
> nor stands in the way of sinners,
>   nor sits in the seat of scoffers. . . . (v. 1)

Community, "the congregation of the righteous" (v. 5), forms the context for nurturing faith. Psalm 2 also deals with the theme of community; it summons communities to choose between life and death, good and evil. God is the one who gives life to communities.

Psalms 12 and 14 show that the community of faith can have problems; most of the community has become unfaithful. These prayers seek liberation for the oppressed. Psalm 3 is an individual lament, but these prayers are always spoken in the context of community. This psalm deals with the problems of fear in the midst of an honest worshiping community, a community with difficulties but with hope in the divine presence.

The Psalter's accent on community bears attention in study and faith. Psalm 133 celebrates the wonder of community; therein are wisdom and blessing:

> Behold, how good and pleasant it is
> when brothers dwell in unity!

It is like the precious oil upon the head,
  running down upon the beard,
upon the beard of Aaron,
  running down on the collar of his robes!
It is like the dew of Hermon,
  which falls on the mountains of Zion!
For there the LORD has commanded the blessing,
  life for evermore.

Providence

The theme of providence, God's providing for ancient Israel, is vital in the Psalms, but it has not received much attention recently. The Psalms speak of God as creating and sustaining life, of God's gracious redeeming acts and the gift of torah, and of God's providing prophets and kings to lead the people.

Psalms 20 and 21 pray for divine providence for the king as he prepares for battle. Verses 6–8 of Psalm 20 convey great confidence in that providence.

Now I know that the LORD will help his anointed;
  he will answer him from his holy heaven
  with mighty victories by his right hand.
Some boast of chariots, and some of horses;
  but we boast of the name of the LORD our God.
They will collapse and fall;
  but we shall rise and stand upright.

Psalm 21 focuses on thanksgiving for providence and victory. The community laments also demonstrate the theme of God's providence. Psalm 67 describes God as the provider of harvest, the one who is present to bring life for the community.

The earth has yielded its increase;
  God, our God has blessed us.
God has blessed us;
  let all the ends of the earth fear him! (vv. 6, 7)

Psalm 124 speaks of the provision of victory or rescue from trouble. Psalm 126 portrays the community seeking a renewal of the past experience of divine providence, a hope for renewal in the new year. Divine providence has a history in the Old Testament, the recounting of which brings hope and help for the future. Psalm 136 tells this story, and its refrain summarizes in traditional Old Testament terms: "for his steadfast love endures for ever." The psalm calls upon the congregation to give thanks for God's providential care seen in creation and deliverance.

Ancient Israel's prayers are infused with affirmations of Yahweh's providence, a major part of the story of God with this community. The Psalms invite the contemporary congregation to enter that story and encounter anew God's provision for life.

Conclusion

Our reflections on the Psalms and faith have brought us back to our framework for studying the Book of Praises: the Psalms function as pilgrimage songs of faith from the depths of human experience. As such these songs sustain the pilgrim community, articulate its common life, and define its faith. The Psalter reveals much of prayer and the life of faith and beckons the contemporary worshiping community to enter its world, a world full of the divine gift of life.

Excursus:
The Psalms and Sociology

Our study of the Psalms has touched on many of the methods used in reading this part of the Old Testament and has suggested that the student of the Psalms can benefit from using each methodology. Old Testament scholars are currently debating over which methods are most appropriate for interpreting the Hebrew Bible. Scholars are thus testing a variety of methods, some of which come from the social sciences. Sociological methods can help us understand the social context from which a text comes as well as the text's impact on society. Learning something of the social standing of those in ancient Israel who produced psalms or who read/heard them can enrich our interpretation of these texts.

We commented in chapter 4 on the work of Walter Brueggemann, who classifies the Psalms with the categories of *orientation*, *disorientation*, and *new orientation*. These categories relate more to social function in the faith community than they do to literary or cultic features. Psalms of *orientation* celebrate security and order in the world; life makes sense. Psalms of *disorientation* (laments) pour forth when the world falls apart and doubt and despair prevail. The *new orientation* expressed in thanksgiving psalms and some hymns remembers the doubt but focuses on a new depth of life found in the struggle.

Norman Gottwald is a leading proponent of the use of sociological methods in Old Testament studies. He has taken up Brueggemann's categories in a summary comment on the Psalms in his introduction to the Hebrew Bible.[1] Gottwald applies the categories to ancient Israelite society. Orientation relates to a just social order, which Gottwald suggests existed when the kings were benevolent and in the time of the tribes before the kings came to power. Mass injustice, whether from rulers within ancient Israel or foreign conquerors, brought on destabilization of community and disorientation. New efforts at justice—reforms, restoration after the Babylonian exile—brought renewed community, renewed orientation.

Gottwald concentrates on the lament psalms. Their language about sufferers and oppressors speaks of socio-economic oppression. Those in power are exploiting the poor and depriving them of goods and rights. The sickness and despair described in the Psalms relate to societal structures that deny the means of well-being for the powerless. Gottwald also contends that the priests, as leaders of the cult, had some power to help victims of the worst societal abuses. The presence in the Psalter of individual thanksgiving psalms implies that the action of oppressors was sometimes blocked. In this way, the cult acted in concert with prophets and with legal provisions that sought to aid the oppressed.

Gottwald's treatment of the Psalms focuses on these texts' relation to societal conflict and to justice. He gives little attention to psalms of praise. Walter Brueggemann's latest volume on the Psalms, however, concentrates on ancient Israel's praise.[2] Brueggemann begins by describing and, appropriately, defending Mowinckel's understanding of cult (liturgy) as the setting of the Psalms. The cult created a "world"—a way of structuring reality—in which the community could live as the people of Yahweh. Ancient Israel's praise was central to that "world." The praise begins with the news of Yahweh's enthronement as king (Psalm 96) but finds its root expression in the liberation of the slaves from

---

[1]N. K. Gottwald, *The Hebrew Bible: A Socio-Literary Introduction* (Philadelphia: Fortress, 1985), 522–41.

[2]W. Brueggemann, *Israel's Praise: Doxology against Idolatry and Ideology* (Philadelphia: Fortress, 1988).

Egypt (Exodus). This vital memory brought hope for the people throughout their history.

This news of the enthronement of the liberating Yahweh was, however, distorted at times under the kings in Jerusalem. Kings often led the people in praising God as one who created the good life to be lived under royal supervision in Jerusalem. The kings were to be participant, sponsor, and benefactor of the cult in Jerusalem. But they were also to be creature, child, and heir of the liturgy; that is, the kings were also to be shaped by the liturgy. The kings were to live in the tension between supervising the cult and being obedient to it. Often, however, they forgot the part of the psalms of praise that remembers Yahweh's liberation of the oppressed and instead simply exploited the cult, and its use of psalms, to their own benefit.

So the kings in their vested interest distorted the "world" created by ancient Israel's praise. Brueggemann discerns signs of this distortion in three features: (1) We saw in chapter 5 that the common style of praise includes summons to praise and reason for the praise. When the reason begins to disappear, the praise is ripe for exploitation by the royal establishment. These psalms simply praise God who supports life as it is. (2) When the language of praise becomes very general rather than specific, the memory of Yahweh as liberator fades. (3) Praise that focuses on creation (order) to the exclusion of transformation (liberation) is an apt tool to support the status quo. This kind of praise describes God as inactive, which is what Brueggemann means by idolatry. It is also a suitable tool for royal exploitation of the people. The praise in the cult proclaims that God supports life as it is under the king; the people should simply submit and obey the whims of the royal establishment. This latter distortion of praise is what Brueggemann means by ideology. Ancient Israel's truest praise, however, like Yahweh, embraces the pain of life. Out of pain the congregation encounters Yahweh's liberating power and offers praise to Yahweh.

Brueggemann has written a formidable work on "Israel's Praise," much of which he relates to the contemporary worshiping community. His position, however, seems somewhat jaundiced, since he is consistently suspicious of creation theology—a view I do not share—and consistently supportive of liberation theology. He understands creation texts inevitably to support an oppressive status quo, that is, the current created order. He reserves the term "ideology" to describe the use of texts in the service of exploitation. Many scholars would argue that ideology is not necessarily a negative term. In fact, the liberation texts Brueggemann treats also imply a certain ideology; they support the position of one group (oppressed) over that of another (oppressors).

Debate will continue over the presuppositions and value of a sociological approach to the Hebrew Bible, but Brueggemann and Gottwald have contributed to our understanding of the Psalms. They have reminded us that disinterested theologies do not exist. Psalms speak of God and of persons; these texts support/oppose numerous groups and societal structures. For example, we have considered the royal psalms. Psalms 2, 110, and 132 certainly endorsed and legitimized the Davidic royal establishment in Jerusalem. At times the monarchy exploited people, as the Old Testament clearly attests; but that does not mean the texts are inherently oppressive. The royal psalms also include Psalms 72 and 101, which speak of the king's responsibilities to bring justice and righteousness. In order to fully encounter a psalm, the student needs to read in sympathy with the text and then put the psalm in its full canonical context.

The hymns of praise also tell of God's support for Zion and the created order centered there. These texts, no doubt, gave legitimacy to the Davidic establishment. These hymns also include texts with prophetic warnings and ethical implications. The psalms of thanksgiving and those recounting God's liberation of the people are also among the hymns. (See chapter 5.) Taken as a whole, the hymns proclaim a "world" that gives life to the human community.

As Gottwald has remarked, the laments support the suffering and oppressed. These texts summon the community to participate with Yahweh in acts of liberation. The contemporary trend to spiritualize the Psalms can lead readers to miss the fact that these texts call the worshiping community to create and support just societal structures. The Psalms do imply vested interests. Considered as a whole, the book's primary interest is fullness of life, a basic component of which is justice. The Psalms declare God's support for justice in the human community.

For Further Reading

Alter, R. *The Art of Biblical Poetry.* New York: Basic Books, 1985.

Anderson, B. *Out of the Depths: The Psalms Speak for Us Today.* Revised and expanded edition. Philadelphia: Westminster, 1983.

Barth, C. *Introduction to the Psalms.* New York: Scribner, 1966.

Brueggemann, W. *The Message of the Psalms: A Theological Commentary.* Minneapolis: Augsburg, 1984.

_____. *Praying the Psalms.* Winona, Minnesota: Saint Mary's Press, 1982.

Crim, K. *The Royal Psalms.* Richmond: John Knox, 1962.

Gunkel, H. *The Psalms.* Facet Books. Philadelphia: Fortress, 1967.

Guthrie, H. *Theology as Thanksgiving.* New York: Seabury, 1981.

Hayes, J. *Understanding the Psalms.* Valley Forge, Pennsylvania: Judson, 1976.

Kraus, H.-J. *Theology of the Psalms.* Minneapolis: Augsburg, 1986.

Lewis, C. S. *Reflections on the Psalms.* New York: Harcourt, Brace & World, 1958.

Miller, P. *Interpreting the Psalms.* Philadelphia: Fortress, 1986.

Mowinckel, S. *The Psalms in Israel's Worship.* 2 volumes. Nashville: Abingdon, 1962.

Weiser, A. *The Psalms. A Commentary.* Old Testament Library. Philadelphia: Westminster, 1962.

Westermann, C. *Praise and Lament in the Psalms.* Atlanta: John Knox, 1981.

_____. *The Psalms.* Minneapolis: Augsburg, 1980.

For Further Study

The purpose of this volume has been not so much to teach about the Psalms as to guide the reader into his or her own study of the Psalms. The following suggestions for study and discussion reflect this goal. The suggestions in part review the material in this volume and ask for further reflection. Some of the tasks invite additional reading.

1. Apply, as an aid for interpretation, the four formative questions of our study (type/structure, use in worship [setting], shaping, rhetoric) to the following psalms: Psalms 13, 46, 72, and 73.

2. Describe the following scholars' contributions to our understanding of the Psalms: Gunkel, Mowinckel, Westermann.

3. Write a brief description of ancient Israel's worship in the temple. Who were the worship leaders? What tasks did they perform?

4. Characterize the writers of the Psalms. Who were the first hearers/readers? Describe them.

5. How did the Psalms originate? Outline the process by which the book of Psalms came together.

6. Make an annotated list of the literary/poetic qualities of the Psalms.

7. What is the significance of Psalm 88?

8. Why is Psalm 109 in the Bible?

9. Describe the message, in its various dimensions, of the lament psalms.

10. What lessons does the Psalter teach concerning the praise of God?

11. The Psalms make use of various images of God, of the speakers of the Psalms, and of the enemies. Write descriptions of the images most significant for you.

12. Articulate a personal view of the theology of the Psalms. How does the book speak to the contemporary community of faith? How do the Psalms relate to contemporary life?

13. How has this study of the Psalms affected your own spiritual pilgrimage?

14. How has this study of the Psalter changed your view of the Psalms?

15. What have you learned from this volume to help you better interpret the Psalms? Describe your own method of studying the Psalms.

16. Apply your method to the following psalms: Psalms 1, 2, 6, and 100.

17. Prepare your own classification of the Psalms. (See the classification in chapter 2.)

Glossary of Names and Terms

Alter, Robert. Professor of Hebrew and comparative literature, University of California, Berkeley. He has written extensively on the literary qualities of the Hebrew Bible, including volumes on the art of biblical narrative and the art of biblical poetry.

Anderson, George W. Emeritus professor of Old Testament, New College, University of Edinburgh. He wrote on a variety of Old Testament topics; the Psalms were of special interest to him.

Babylonian Exile. The imprisonment of the people of ancient Israel in Babylon (587–538 BC). This traumatic experience began with the destruction of Jerusalem, a blow which effectively spelled the end of ancient Israel as a nation. Various parts of the Old Testament reflect the impact of the exile. The Persians conquered the Babylonians and allowed the Jews to return home.

Balla, Emil. Old Testament scholar in Germany in the first part of the twentieth century. His work reflects the influence of his teacher Hermann Gunkel. Balla provided the basic support for the view that the "I" of the Psalms was an individual rather than the nation personified.

Begrich, Joachim. Old Testament scholar and a student of Gunkel who worked in Germany in the first part of the twentieth century. Upon Gunkel's death, Begrich completed his teacher's mammoth introduction to the Psalms (1933).

Bentzen, Aage. Professor of Old Testament, University of Copenhagen, until the middle of this century. A number of his studies have appeared in English translation, including *King and Messiah*. Bentzen's work is representative of Scandinavian Old Testament scholarship.

Birkeland, Harris. Scandinavian Old Testament scholar and a student of Mowinckel. He supported the view that the enemies in the Psalms were national enemies. Most of his work came between 1930 and 1955.

Brueggemann, Walter. Old Testament professor, Columbia Theological Seminary, Decatur, Ga. He has written extensively on various biblical themes and their relevance to contemporary life. Brueggemann classified the Psalms in terms of orientation (all is right with the world), disorientation (the world is falling apart), and new orientation (the world has been formed anew but, because of the experience of disorientation, is no longer taken for granted).

Childs, Brevard. Old Testament scholar, Yale University. His work has stirred significant debate on the canonical context of the Old Testament. "Canon" signifies the books included in the Old Testament and their place as authority for life and faith. Scholars have often concentrated on how the books originated, but Childs argues that we should study the Old Testament in its present canonical form.

Clements, Ronald. Professor of Old Testament, King's College, University of London. He has written extensively on the book of Isaiah, Old Testament theology, and the history of Old Testament scholarship.

Cult. The organized worship of ancient Israel conducted primarily, though not exclusively, in the Jerusalem temple.

Davidic Covenant. The divine promise to David that he and his sons would rule over the people in Jerusalem. A primary expression of the promise is in 2 Samuel 7.

Eaton, John. Old Testament scholar, University of Birmingham, England. His writings concentrate on Old Testament worship and the place of the king in that worship.

Elohim. The Hebrew word for "God." The term can mean "god, gods, divine beings" but in the Old Testament, it most often refers to the one God of ancient Israel.

Festivals, Old Testament. Periodic times of worship and celebration in connection with the Jerusalem temple. The history of these festivals is difficult to piece together, but the Old Testament does speak of such special occasions. The Feasts of Passover, Weeks, and Tabernacles reminded the people of God's gifts of harvest and revelation and of God's delivering Israel from slavery in Egypt. Leviticus 23 connects the Feast of Tabernacles with New Year's and with the Day of Atonement (Leviticus 16). The ritual of the Day of Atonement provided a means of renewing the broken relationship with God.

Gunkel, Hermann. Significant Old Testament scholar in Germany in the early twentieth century (died in 1932). Gunkel wrote numerous Old Testament studies. He is the originator of form criticism, the historical analysis of the various kinds of Old Testament literature. His studies provide a major beginning point for contemporary Psalms scholarship.

Israel/Judah. The Hebrew kingdoms. The nation of ancient Israel was a united kingdom under Kings Saul, David, and Solomon. At Solomon's death (922 BC), the kingdom split into the northern kingdom of Israel, sometimes called Ephraim after its major tribe, and the southern kingdom of Judah.

Johnson, Aubrey. Old Testament professor, University College, Cardiff, Wales, in the last generation. Johnson wrote several volumes on the relationship, in the Old Testament, between king, prophet, and worship.

Maccabean. Family which led the Jewish revolt in the second century BC. The revolt overthrew oppressive rulers. The Jews remained independent, with Maccabean leaders, until the coming of the Roman Empire.

Miller, Patrick. Old Testament professor, Princeton Theological Seminary. Miller has written on the ancient Near Eastern background of the Old Testament and on the Psalms.

Mowinckel, Sigmund. Old Testament scholar, University of Oslo, and a student of Gunkel. He wrote, between 1920 and 1960, many influential studies on topics such as Old Testament worship, the Psalms, and the book of Jeremiah.

Rhetoric. The persuasive use of language. Texts employ a variety of literary devices, such as repetition, to convince readers/hearers. An analysis of these devices may thus help with the task of interpretation.

Righteous. Faithful to a relationship. In the Old Testament, righteousness does not refer to morally right acts so much as to right relationship. The righteous are those who act in fidelity to their relationship with God. God is righteous in that God acts to bring people into right relationships.

Sennacherib. Assyrian ruler who led an invasion of Judah and laid siege to Jerusalem in 701 BC.

Shaping. The molding of the book of Psalms into its final form as a prayer book for the faith community. The Psalter came about through a process, and in that process, the community—through its worship leaders and theologians—shaped the Psalms in such a way as to aid the people's life of faith and worship. This shaping included redacting, or editing, individual psalms and organizing the whole Psalter.

Sheol. The realm of the dead. The Old Testament generally takes the view that upon death one enters the shadowy, murky world of the dead, the underworld. Death is also an active, debilitating power which can invade life. Thus the Psalms speak of being gripped by the power of Sheol.

Smend, Rudolf. German Old Testament scholar in the late nineteenth century. He proposed that the "I" in the Psalms often personified the nation of Israel.

Versions, Old Testament. Translations of the Hebrew Bible. Of particular importance are the ancient translations into Greek (Septuagint), Syriac (Peshitta), and Latin (Vulgate).

Weiser, Artur. Professor of Old Testament, University of Tübingen, West Germany, in the middle of this century. Weiser produced a number of Old Testament studies. He especially emphasized the importance of ancient Israel's covenant renewal in the Psalms.

Westermann, Claus. Emeritus Professor of Old Testament, University of Heidelberg, West Germany. His works on Genesis, the Psalms, Job, the Prophets, and Old Testament theology have been particularly influential.

Wisdom Literature. The parts of the Old Testament produced by ancient Israel's wisdom teachers. Proverbs, Job, and Ecclesiastes are the main books. They explore the meaning of life and give advice for daily living.

Yahweh. The special Old Testament name for God. The proper noun is written as four Hebrew letters יהוה (*Yhwh*). The community eventually stopped saying the name because it was so sacred; they substituted either the word for God or the word for Lord. Thus there has been confusion about the vowel sounds in the name. "Jehovah" derives from this confusion, but Yahweh is a more likely pronunciation. Most English versions translate the name "LORD." Exodus 3 holds special importance for the significance of the name.

Zion. Jerusalem and its temple. The temple was the special place of God's presence with ancient Israel and the city a special symbol of the kingdom. The life-giving worship at the sanctuary was of central import for the community; pilgrims came there to participate in regular and festival worship. The entrance liturgies relate to the ritual in which pilgrims ask who may enter the temple to worship. The priest answers that the one who lives a moral life may enter. Yahweh's enthronement as king was also celebrated in the Jerusalem temple (enthronement psalms).

Index of Names

Scripture Index